Robina Napier

Field-Marshal Count Moltke's Letters from Russia

Robina Napier

Field-Marshal Count Moltke's Letters from Russia

ISBN/EAN: 9783337309824

Printed in Europe, USA, Canada, Australia, Japan

Cover: Foto ©ninafisch / pixelio.de

More available books at **www.hansebooks.com**

FIELD-MARSHAL COUNT MOLTKE'S
Letters from Russia

Translated by
ROBINA NAPIER

LONDON
C. KEGAN PAUL & CO., 1, PATERNOSTER SQUARE
1878

[The rights of translation and of reproduction are reserved.]

INTRODUCTORY NOTICE.

AT THE beginning of the year 1866, the German people were unaware that it had in its army the greatest military genius of the age.

The silent, retiring officer who was at that time Chief of the Staff at Berlin, had reached the age of sixty-six years without doing much to attract the notice of the world. The King knew him, and the army had instinctive confidence in him from the first, but not till Königgrätz did Germany know what she possessed in General Von Moltke. Placed by that brilliant success on the summit of military fame, he became an object of interest to the whole German people. His portrait was in every shop window, and a history of his life in

Introductory Notice

every magazine. Photography ensured a certain accuracy in the portraits, which was too often wanting in the biographies. The man, however, who had gained the popular epithet of "*The Silent*" was not likely to speak of himself; and war and misfortune had left him the sole representative of an ancient house. That nothing was known of his history did not prevent a great deal being written.

It was, therefore, a bold and happy thought which prompted a correspondent of the popular journal called "*Daheim*," to wait upon the great man himself and beg for information.

Moltke is no longer merely German, he has grown to be one of those of whom the world is proud, though we in England know him now no more than Germany did then. It will, therefore, probably be acceptable to give some account of an interview which brought out so much that was interesting, and to collect also a few further particulars.

The "*Visit to General Von Moltke*" is described

Introductory Notice.

in the October number of "*Daheim*" for 1866. The correspondent, who merely signs himself "*M.*," relates that "friendly introductions having preceded him," he went, in some trepidation at the boldness of the step he had taken, to present himself at the house of the General of the Staff, No. 66 Behren Strasse, in Berlin. He was immediately admitted, and conducted to the General's private room or study. The first impression made by Moltke is that of extreme gravity; his tall, upright figure seems born to command; the expression of his features is that of iron firmness, the wrinkles on his face appeared to be chiselled on a block of marble.

General von Moltke received his visitor with great politeness, and to his request to furnish him with some details of his history, he replied —"You are very much mistaken in coming to me if you think that my life will furnish any of those brilliant descriptions dear to poets and to the general public. My life is so poor in episodes that it would be considered quite tedious, and I do not see how my biography should contain anything but dates."

Herr Dr. *M.* replied that a man's life is sometimes more interesting to a stranger than to himself; to which Moltke assented, and after a time proceeded, "I will tell you exactly what I feel: I have an antipathy for *praise-mongering*, such as some persons have for certain animals. It puts me out of tune for a whole day to hear anything of the kind. The Bohemian campaign is, indeed, a grand undying page in the history of the world, an event the consequences of which no one—*no one* can now foresee. I have done my duty and filled my position honourably, like all my comrades—nothing more. God's almighty power has guided the victorious flight of the Prussian eagle. The bravery of our army, the caution of their leaders, as well as my plans, are only the instruments of His will; and when I hear the boundless laudations which the public heap on me, the thought always recurs, How would it have

Introductory Notice. ix

been if success, this unparalleled success, had not crowned our efforts? would not the unmerited praises of so many ignorant critics have become just so much unmerited blame? However," he continued, after a time, "I shall willingly give you the particulars you desire for your journal, and you can rectify a mistake which has been made as to the place of my birth."

The conversation was continued for an hour and a half; then his visitor, feeling that he ought to go, rose to take leave.

"And now, poor man, are you going to sit down after you leave me and write down all our conversation?" to which his visitor replied "Yes, your Excellency; and I only wish that I could give this memorable conversation word for word."

"But how is that possible? How can you give all the dates and details I have told you?" to which Dr. *M.* replied that he could but do his best, and that readers must pardon any

Introductory Notice.

trivial errors he might fall into. The General then said abruptly, but in a pleasant tone of voice, "Do you know, I like the boldness of the step you have taken,—it was right, and deserves the approbation of your readers; you will write of me *de visu*, and what you say of me will not be a mere fancy portrait. But I am really sorry for you when I consider that the slightest error in your work, the least failure of memory, will be judged as harshly as if you had written merely from hearsay! But what is to be done?" Then, seeing his visitor silent and confused, he continued with a pleasant smile, "I will try and help you myself."

And so he did! for a few days after, when Dr. *M.*, though full of the general impression of the great man, was beginning to despair of reproducing the conversation with anything like accuracy, a small packet was placed in his hands containing notes in the handwriting of Moltke himself! Many of these notes referred to strictly military details, but in the following

Introductory Notice. xi

sketch we shall reproduce all that is of a personal character or of general interest.

"I am the third of the seven sons of my father, who was a Lieutenant-General in the Danish army. My mother was Henrietta Paschen, the daughter of the Finanz-Rath of Hamburg. Although my parents resided first in Priegnitz and then in Mecklenburg, I was born at Parchim, October 26, 1800, when they were visiting my uncle Helmuth von Moltke. I was baptised Helmuth Karl Bernhardt. I went with my parents to Lübeck, where, in 1806, our house was plundered by the French. My earliest recollections are connected with that old city and its gates and towers, and I recognised our house in the '*Schrangen*' after many long years, in spite of its altered surroundings.

"In the meantime my father had bought a country house in Holstein, which, the year after, was burnt down just after the grain had been gathered in. Soon after this my grandfather died. By his will he left many very large legacies, and owing to the heavy and unforeseen losses caused by the war, my mother, who was his heiress, was left so burdened that the property had to be sold. Meanwhile my eldest brother and I were sent to the Cadet School at Copenhagen. There we passed a joyless boyhood. At eighteen I became an officer. The small prospect which the Danish service offered led me to wish to enter the Prussian service, in which my father and his brothers had served. I therefore went to Berlin, taking with me good recommendations from the Duke of Holstein-Beck, the father of the present King of Denmark. I passed the examination and entered the infantry regiment No. 8. There began my military career, the course of which is sufficiently known."

In the year 1811 Helmuth von Moltke and his brother Fritz were placed under the care of Pastor Knickbein at Hohenfield near Horst. In this quiet country place, under the kindly

Introductory Notice.

care of a good and amiable man, the boys grew in health and vigour. Their favourite amusement was the "*Kriegspiel*," or mimic warfare, in which they were great proficients.

On one occasion the two brothers put themselves at the head of a number of peasant boys, the battlefield being a stubble enclosed by a high fence. Helmuth's troop was put to flight, and some were made prisoners in getting over the hedge, but quickly rallying his men he marched them straight to a pond in the pastor's garden, where he pointed out a little island, accessible only by a drawbridge made of a single plank. The embryo field-marshal then turned on the enemy with a few of his strongest men, and kept him at bay while the rest of his forces made their way into the fortress. When all had entered, he himself being the last, the drawbridge was raised and the victory was complete. The pastor and the boys' father came up just in time to enjoy the scene. The island in the pond had been made by Helmuth with great labour, out of materials collected from all directions, but whether it was done merely for the amusement of the time, or with the intention of using it for military purposes, is not known.

This "*Moltke Island*" became a favourite resort of Pastor Knickbein, who had it planted in honour of the quiet and clever pupil, who has since become so famous. Nor did the scholar forget his master, for when, thirty years afterwards, he published his first work, "*Letters from Turkey*," he sent a copy to the pastor with this inscription, "*To my dear Friend and Teacher, to whom I owe so much, I send this, my first production, as a slight token of respect.*"

To these happy years in Höhenfeld succeeded some very unhappy ones in Copenhagen, where the boys went in 1812 to attend the school for Cadets. Their father placed them under the charge of General Lorenz, who was a bachelor, and left all the management of the house to his old housekeeper, seeing the boys only at meal times. In due time they

Introductory Notice. xv

were removed to the Cadet school-house; but although they escaped from the ill-natured old housekeeper, their position was far from pleasant, as Moltke himself thus describes it:—

"Our boyhood, in a foreign city without relations or friends, was truly miserable. The discipline was strict, even severe; and now, when my judgment of it is quite impartial, I must say that it was too strict, too severe. The only good which this treatment did for us, was that we were early obliged to accustom ourselves to privations of every kind. Yet this discipline had perhaps its good side, if it were only that it filled me with perpetual thankfulness to a family in Copenhagen who were most kind and friendly to us. General Hegermann Lindencrone had a beautiful country house near the town, which was the scene of our boyish games, when we went there on Sunday with his three sons, who afterwards entered the Danish army. The intercourse with the refined and cultivated members of this family had, I assure you, a most salutary effect on my whole after-life. Parents sending their sons into such a school cannot be too strongly urged to recommend them to the notice of some cultivated family. I know the effect in myself."

The boys remained under this strict discipline for six years, and indeed the course would have been longer, but for their great diligence and talent. Helmuth particularly distinguished himself, especially in all the literary and scientific branches of military study. At the final examination he took a first class, and gained the rank of lieutenant. One who was his comrade at this school thus describes him as he was then:—"He was a slender young fellow with a quantity of fair hair, good-natured blue eyes, very quiet, of pleasing and engaging manners; his countenance was open and genial, but there was occasionally an expression of deep melancholy. His unwearied diligence and energetic determination shrank from no task, and his firm will carried him successfully through everything

Introductory Notice.

which he attempted. His comrades had a great respect for him, but though he was aware of it he never asserted himself in the least: in conversation he was communicative and animated, on duty or at work he was quiet and unobtrusive. His zeal for duty was untiring, and his power of attaining knowledge quite unequalled."

On leaving the Cadet School the brothers were pages at the court for a year, and at the end of that time, in 1819, Helmuth was appointed lieutenant in a regiment stationed at Rendsburg.

But after the separation of Denmark from Norway, the reduction of the army condemned nearly all the officers to remain in attendance at court, and every regiment being over-officered, there was no hope of promotion for the younger men. Young Moltke, however, was ambitious, and he saw that promotion was only possible in a large army, and as the Prussian army had gained a great reputation in the War of Liberation, he determined to retire from the Danish and enter the Prussian service. Although he knew that by so doing he would lose the benefit of the four years he had served in the Danish army, and also have to undergo another examination; this done, he entered a Prussian regiment stationed at Frankfort. The following year he went to the great military academy at Berlin, and remained there till 1826.

"The first part of my career was destitute of the joys of life. I left the Kriegs-Schule in Berlin at a time when my parents had lost almost the whole of their property from war and misfortune. Not one penny could they give me, and you can hardly imagine how pinched I was. In spite of this, however, I contrived to spare enough to get instruction in foreign languages—but this was a very difficult operation. . . . The lot of a poor lieutenant indeed is unenviable!"

"While I was at Frankfort I became acquainted with the family of General von der Marwitz, whose wife was a distant relation of ours. I found in this house not only a friendly

Introductory Notice.

reception, but enjoyed also the most beneficial intellectual intercourse. I think I see before me the excellent General—he was the most polite man in the world; when any one came in, he immediately took off his little cap and laid it on the paper just before him. Yes! the politest man in the world—and he once gave the young Lieutenant—I mean myself—a severe lesson which he has never forgotten. You cannot imagine how deep two words sank into my mind, driving all the blood into my face! I went to see him one day, and as I have said, he took off his little cap and put it on the sheet of paper before him, and with a pleasant smile invited me to come in. With the greatest good humour I laid my shako down on a chair, and taking off my sword I was just about to set it up in the nearest corner, when the General said quietly but very sharply, 'In the ante-room, *Herr Lieutenant*; may I beg you, sir, in the ante-room!' Do not laugh, but I assure you that I still feel myself grow quite red whenever I think of this well-deserved reprimand."

In 1832, Moltke was appointed to the staff, and continued in that service for three years, during which time his extraordinary powers of combination and organisation were developed by the scientific and exact nature of his studies. At the end of three years he obtained leave to travel, in order to satisfy his craving to see something of foreign lands. He bent his step first to Turkey, setting out in October 1835, but did not arrive in Constantinople till December, the journey being at that time one of considerable difficulty. Mahmoud II., who was then Sultan, had just undertaken the work of reconstructing the Turkish army after the European models. He had tried in vain to induce either English or French officers to help him to do this, and as Moltke arrived at the very moment, he was gladly welcomed and entrusted with the task. During his residence in Constantinople he made surveys for a general plan of that city, and when this work was finished in 1837, he visited several places on the Asiatic coast. In his capacity of military adviser also he accompanied the Sultan on a visit to Bulgaria and Roumelia.

During the next two years he was not only employed in the reorganisation of the Turkish army, but he actually accompanied an expedition against the Pasha of Egypt. The Turkish commander, however, refused to be advised by Moltke, and in consequence he met with a disastrous defeat at Nisib. Moltke and two Russian officers who were with him, escaped with difficulty to a port on the Black Sea, whence he made his way back to Constantinople, where, however, he only remained long enough to explain the disaster to the Sultan, and exculpate himself from all share in it. He then, in October 1839, returned to his old position in Berlin.

While Moltke was in Turkey, he described

everything he saw, and all that happened to him, in letters to his sister. This lady had married an Englishman who resided in Holstein, Mr. Burt, a widower, with one daughter. The letters, interesting as they are to ordinary readers, even at this distance of time, must have been fascinating indeed to the little household which received them, and it is not surprising that the interest they excited in this young lady, the stepdaughter of his sister, just then growing into womanhood, should have prepared her to take a still warmer interest in the writer himself.

Shortly after his return to Berlin, Major von Moltke obtained leave to visit his sister, and under her roof formed the acquaintance which ended in Mary Burt becoming his wife. They were married in 1845, and the next year Moltke was appointed Adjutant-in-Attendance on Prince Henry of Prussia, the king's uncle, a constant invalid, who lived in Rome. Here he remained with his wife for two years, employing his abundant leisure in making plans and maps of the city and neighbourhood, as well as sketches, of which he himself says, "My *Contorni di Roma*" were engraved, and I have received many commendations of them from high quarters."

After the Prince's death, in 1847, he returned to Berlin, and was soon afterwards made Chief of the Staff of the 8th division of the army, then at Coblentz. In the summer of 1856 he visited Russia in attendance on the Crown Prince, and it was then that he wrote the letters to his wife which form the present volume. In the same year, still in attendance on the Crown Prince, he was present at the betrothal of that Prince to the Princess Royal of England at Balmoral; in fact, he has visited England with the Prince three or four times.

In the year 1858 Moltke was made Chief of the General Staff in Berlin, and forthwith began with von Roon, the war minister, the reorganisation of the Prussian army, a labour, the results of which astonished the world eight years afterwards. He elaborated plans also for the defence of the German coasts and the creation of a German navy.

Though General von Moltke served with distinction in the war with Denmark in 1864, he had no opportunity of showing his great powers till the war between Prussia and Austria in 1866. The course of that war and its splendid success is too well known to need repetition. He himself calls it "a campaign which for Prussia, for Germany, and for the whole world, has an importance which it is impossible to measure."

But this brilliant success was shortly followed by the great sorrow of his life. On Christmas Eve, 1868, his wife died, leaving him, after twenty-three years of happy married life, without any child.

Sorrow, however, did not prevent Moltke from fulfilling the duties of his high position. Every political observer in Germany felt that

Introductory Notice.

sooner or later war with France was inevitable, and he quietly worked out the plans for a campaign against France. It was not long before these were wanted, and the great soldier was soon drawn from the retirement of Kreisau in Silesia, where he lingered by the grave of his wife, to sterner duties. At the first news of the coming storm Moltke and Bismarck hastened to Berlin, and then begun that terrible conflict which ended in a German Empire victorious and united. True and memorable are the words which the noble King spoke at the great banquet, held after the battle of Sedan, in drinking to his brave army : "You, von Roon, have sharpened my sword; you, General von Moltke, have wielded it; and you, Count von Bismarck have guided the policy of Prussia for years towards the height which it has this day attained."

The close relations which existed between the King and his faithful servants, Moltke the great soldier, and Bismarck the great statesman, are exemplified by a circumstance which is said to have occurred at the end of the terrible conflict at Gravelotte, is very characteristic. The Pomeranians having come up just at the right time, as arranged by Moltke, the French were defeated and driven into Metz. It was late in the evening when the victory was decided, and as it was impossible for them to return to the headquarters at Pont à Mousson, so the King and his immediate followers were obliged to seek shelter in Rezonville, or spend the night in the open air. All the houses were filled with the wounded; only one small room was found for the King, and here a camp-bed was brought for his Majesty. "And where is Moltke, where is Bismarck to be quartered?" asked the King. "Nowhere at present," said the adjutant. "Fetch them here," said the King, sending away the camp-bed for the use of the wounded, and ordered some straw to be brought, of which a bed was made, on which the King, Moltke, and Bismarck slept all three together.

Introductory Notice.

He took the motto, "*march separately, strike together*," and this rule, carried out with his marvellous power of combination and organisation, produced the greatest results. Not only has he a wonderfully clear intellect, seizing the point of everything before him, but he has the power of making others understand his plans, and see the probability of his presuppositions, and the justice of his conclusions. Reticence and modesty are among his notorious characteristics, and while the popular idea of him, at least in England, is much more stern than the letters warrant us in accepting, he bears well the ancient Latin motto of the Moltke family, "*Caute et candide.*"

This slight sketch of a great man's life may well be concluded with his own words—true words—when they were uttered in 1866, how much more so in 1877!

"Yes, indeed! it is beautiful when God lights up the evening of a man's life as he has done that of King William and many of his generals.

Introductory Notice.

I, too, am sixty-six years, and I have received a reward for my life's labours such as very few attain. . . . However hard may have been the struggles of our early life, yet verily after this campaign we old people may boast ourselves the darlings of Fortune."

But Count von Moltke is also an author. *The Letters from Turkey* published in 1835 was his first and is the most popular of his works. The *Introduction* is written by Karl Ritter, the well-known geographer. A German critic has said, in speaking of the descriptions contained in these letters, " His language is so vivid in its colouring and his style so elevated, that we are tempted to say, if Moltke had not become Moltke, he would certainly have been a poet !"

In the same year he published an historical account of *The Campaign in Turkey*, of which he said to the correspondent of *"Daheim,"* " I daresay you have never heard of it. It appeared anonymously, like all my books, and it must have been what you call a literary *fiasco*, for I have never heard any but professional men speak of it."

His book on the *Italian Campaign of* 1859, published in 1863, made a great sensation in Austria, especially on account of the high estimation in which he holds the character of General Benedek.

The history of the *German and French War of* 1870-71, published by the General Staff in Berlin in 1874, was of course written entirely under his direction, and it is said that the greater part of it is actually from his pen.

The Letters from Russia which form the present volume were written by Count von Moltke to his wife, then residing in Copenhagen, when he attended Prince Friedrich Wilhelm, now Crown Prince of Germany, at the coronation of the Emperor of Russia. By an unexplained, but happy accident, they found their way, in a Danish dress, into the

d

pages of a Copenhagen journal "*Dagens Myheder*," and were translated into Danish and published. Though read with great interest in Denmark, they were little noticed in Germany till February 1877, when they were retranslated from the Danish and published in the "*Deutsche Rundshau.*" They necessarily suffered in these transfusions, and Count von Moltke was asked to allow the publication of the originals. The permission was granted with the proviso that the profits of the sale were to be applied to the fund for the wounded soldiers in the war of 1870-71. The little volume was well received, and a second edition soon called for, from which the present translation has been made.

In these letters the writer's wonderful talent for observation is seen in the description of the most minute details, which gives them a charming frehsness and vivacity. They also contain some remarkable reflections on the life of the Russian people, both public and private, which are applicable to the Russia of the present.

Introductory Notice.

day, notwithstanding the great reforms introduced by the Emperor. They are, however, chiefly interesting for the pleasing side-lights they throw on the character of this great man.

R. N.

HOLKHAM VICARAGE,
    Jan. 1, 1878.

Count Moltke's Letters from Russia.

PETERHOF, *Friday*, *August* 15, 1856.

FROM the weather in which we left Berlin we had reason to expect a very bad passage; but, in reality, we made an excellent one. You would, I hope, receive my pencil note from Swinemünde early on Wednesday. Even by the time we arrived at that port the wind had somewhat abated, and when I saw the two great war-steamers which were to convey us, I thought to myself that very big waves indeed would be required to disturb their dignified calm.

The Empress was some time in bidding farewell to her sisters, and we took advantage of the interval to settle ourselves on board the corvette "Grämeschtschik" (the "Thunderer"). About seven o'clock the king embarked in the

"Nagler," which then shot past us to her position in front. The Russian sailors manned the yards, the band struck up, and the moment of our departure had arrived. The first thing necessary was to turn the bows of the two leviathans towards Russia. The channel was so narrow that this could not be accomplished with their own paddles, and the little tug had to take out first one and then the other of these monsters. But as soon as they were once in the right position they paddled away between the moles, more than a thousand feet long, to the open sea.

I had then to give myself up to my fate, and determined to fortify myself against all accidents by eating a very good dinner before I retired to my cabin.

"*Faites un peu amarrer vos effets,*" was the excellent advice which was given me. My "*hotel*" had a front window; but this did little to throw light into my miserable cabin, for it was merely a small square of thick green glass. The furniture was simple indeed, and might be said to consist of the chain belonging to the rudder, which was in constant movement, creaking perpetually in the most frightful manner.

Bedclothes were not to be thought of, so I wrapped myself up in my cloak, as if I had been camping out, threw myself on the "*couchette,*" and slept in sound and unbroken sleep till daybreak.

My awaking in the cold grey morning was not very agreeable. "*Je suis fâché de vous dire qu'il y ait de moutons,*" was the salutation of General Philosophof, who did the honours of the "Thunderer" in the most polite manner possible. These "*moutons*" are in fact the great waves crested with foam which are the precursors of heavy gales.

I gave myself up to melancholy reflections, and in three times four-and-twenty hours one has time for a great many. From both sides came the most mournful sounds, through the thin wooden partitions which separated me from my companions in misery. I was incapable of taking even a cup of coffee, and in order to escape from the disagreeable atmosphere of the cabin, I dragged myself up on deck.

Frederick had lain since yesterday in the last

extremity, and I summoned up all my linguistic powers with the addition of an expressive pantomime, to interest Murawief, the ship boy, in my helpless condition. They brought me a mattress on deck, and I took the only means of overcoming sea-sickness, namely, to lie still and bear it.

With every hour I got better. The wind, too, went down, and the vessel was so broad, that the roll was but little felt. By mid-day I had read half of a French novel, which the benevolent Prince Trubetzkoi had brought me from Paris. Towards evening I made some feeble attempts at walking, having fasted the whole day. I slept well this second night, in spite of the smell of tallow and the constant movement of the ship.

In the morning I took my coffee with fear and trembling, and at eleven o'clock, with some qualms, I ventured on herring, cold meat, and red wine; then with more boldness attacked an excellent dinner. Old Malaga, good Lafitte, and *champagne frappé* helped down the *cotelettes truffées* and artichokes, which might otherwise have been too much for me.

In the evening it was impossible to refuse the incomparable caravan tea, from Kiachta, and all this succeeded so well, that I even risked a supper, at which I drank your health in champagne, saying to myself at the same time, that you might be thinking anxiously of me, at that very moment when I was so elegantly emptying my glass. So contentment is often found where we do not expect it, even in a rolling vessel, whilst despair and bitter sorrow sometimes waltz beneath the brilliant chandeliers of the ball room.

This *vendredi gras* was also rich in many interesting occurrences. Before noon we approached the "Olaf" so closely that we were able to exchange salutations with the other members of the suite.

The Empress caused inquiries to be made after our health, to which we answered, of course, that our health was most excellent, and we begged to be informed of the health of Her Majesty. The answer was, "to-day, thank God, very well;" from which we concluded that yesterday her Majesty had been ill.

This little correspondence was carried on

by means of thirty or forty flags of different colours run up to the mainmast. By and by we passed a great Russian man-of-war from the coast of Finland, which saluted the Imperial flag by a rolling fire from both her decks. The "Thunderer" returned thanks for the "Olaf" in thirty-one mighty words which issued from her brazen mouths. The whole made a very pretty picture.

As soon as the sun set, the wind subsided, the full moon shone through streaky clouds, the air became mild and soft, and the waves murmured gently.

Every half-hour the "Olaf" burned a Bengal light, to which our vessel replied by a signal of the same kind. This was done to make sure that the little "Gremäschtschik" was neither too near nor too far away from the "Olaf." I remained on deck till two o'clock.

This has been a most beautiful sunshiny day. On either side islands surmounted with their lighthouses, and then the narrowing shores, broke on our sight. The farther we advanced into the Bay of Finland the smoother was the sea, but as we were afraid of arriving before the Emperor expected us, we steamed for the greater part of the time at half speed.

At noon I counted more than two hundred sail, the light breeze from the north enabling vessels to leave the port of Cronstadt. Soon afterwards the northern Venice rose above the sea. Enormous fortifications of freestone with three lines of casemates and fortified platforms are placed on many little islands, and there is quite a forest of masts in the harbour of the merchantmen. Behind towered the masts of the great men-of-war, which even "fighting Charlie" could not entice from their immovable calm, though he lay right opposite to them, almost within the range of their guns.

It was very easy for us to form an accurate idea of the reception he and his "hearts of oak" would have met with, if they had approached a little nearer, for as soon as the "Olaf" was about two thousand feet from the fortress, thick white clouds issued from every tower, casemate, and battery, and then a roll of thunder which quite overpowered the sound of our own cannonade, although that was severe enough to make our vessel tremble under it. An English eighty gun-ship, which was lying at anchor, joined merrily in the concert. This ship had made use of the sunshine to have a great wash, and the shirts and trousers of her crew, in every shade of colour were hung out to dry. As the arrival of the Empress was undoubtedly known, this was a proof of " Johnny Bull's" careless ease.

An extremely small steam vessel with two funnels now shot past us, having on board the High Admiral, the Prince Constantine,* and the Emperor,† who hastened to meet his mother.

It had been thought hardly possible that this noble lady's delicate health would allow her to return from Wildbad Gastein in Tyrol to the Neva; but she had determined to bestow her blessing on her son at his coronation, according to the beautiful old custom of this country, even if she should die in consequence. And what this lady wills, she wills decidedly.

Of course we were all on deck in full dress, and immediately afterwards boarded the small

* Brother of Emperor Alexander II. of Russia, born 1827.

† Alexander II., born 1818, crowned September 7 1856.

vessel of the Russian Admiral, the "St. Petersburg."

Fancy if all this grand reception had taken place in different circumstances, on a rainy day, with a high sea, with fits of sea-sickness, and you will acknowledge that our situation would have been horrible! But the reality was beautiful, and we glided swiftly over a mirror-like sea, to the adjacent coast. On the horizon, to the left, shone something, which, if it were not the middle of the day, might have been taken for a star. It was the gilded cupola of the Isaac Church in Petersburg.

We soon landed on the fine broad steps of Peterhof; the Empress had already passed on between the lines of troops, surrounded by an epauletted crowd, blazing with stars and gorgeous uniforms. We were, however, presently seized upon by a liveried servant who placed us in a cab, which carried us past a row of fountains to the palace, and thence to our apartment, where a swarm of servants and equipages stood at our disposal.

And now that I have come happily to land, and it is ten o'clock, I will conclude for to-day, wishing you heartily good night. My letter will not go much before mid-day, so that I can continue my account in the morning before my land impressions have overcome my maritime reminiscences. After having passed three nights without taking off my clothes, an elegant bed with good mattresses and silken quilt, smiles upon me most pleasantly.

Letters from Russia.

Saturday, August 16.

THE grand palace of Peterhof, built by Peter I. and enlarged by his daughter Elizabeth, is, like St. James's Palace, used only for receptions. In the extensive park which surrounds it, lie villas and mansions now occupied by the Imperial family and their guests. Prince Hohenzollern, Heinz, Katte, and I, lodge in one of these houses for the present.

I have a large and pretty room, with a very pleasant green outlook, and, which is priceless in this damp cold region, on the sunny side of the house. Yet spite of this, I was glad of my cloak during the night.

Immediately on our arrrival I received visits from Count Münster, and Adjutant Von Mirbach, who has been appointed to attend the Prince.* The dinner was undress (frock coats without swords). I found there our ambassador Werther, the young Count Werther-Beuchlingen, whom you know, and after dinner there was a general presentation and introduction.

* Frederick William, present Crown Prince of Germany.

We took our coffee on the balcony in front of the castle, from which can be seen the beautiful fountains, which play before all the more important parts of the building, and which have the great merit of rising from natural springs instead of being made to play artificially by steam power.

After dinner, I had only to lift my finger, and up jumped the Iswoschtschik to his seat, seized the single rein with out-stretched hands, threw back his body, and off we went in the open droschke at a sharp trot through the extensive grounds of Peterhof.

Archimedes sought for a *point d'appui* beyond the earth, by which to move the earth out of its orbit. Peter the Great made a *point d'appui* for his reforms beyond his kingdom, in the Swedish provinces conquered by him. There he built his European capital, and when it was finished he constructed Peterhof, from whence he could see how Petersburg looked.

The palace is a rather large three-storeyed building, in the French style. It is connected by galleries with two pavilions. The colour, yellow and white, harmonises with the leadening of the roofs and the exceedingly rich gilding of the cupolas. The building stands on a terrace about forty feet high, formed by the natural slope of the mainland towards the Bay of Finland. There is a space between the castle and the sea of about one thousand feet, which is occupied by the park. In a direct line from the middle of the palace there is a large basin, made of stone-work, and leading to the steps which form the landing-place from the sea. On both sides of this basin is a row of fountains, thus forming an alley of *jets d'eau* — in the highest degree singular. The drives run along the side of these fountains, surrounded with tall dark fir-trees, between which one looks over this foreground towards the sea, with the coast of Finland appearing quite on the horizon. The whole makes a most surprising and charming impression.

 The park also is very beautiful, and takes its peculiar character from its countless waterworks. The highest jets, those which are before the grotto in the middle of the castle, are, however, not more than fifty or sixty feet high, and are not thicker than one's arm, so that they are not to be compared to those of Wilhelmshöhe or Sans-Souci, but their number is endless. Everywhere under the shade of the trees, among temples and statues, the splashing and murmuring of the water in cascades and basins is heard.

The turf is certainly not like the natural velvet of Windsor, or the artificial velvet of Glienicke,* but still it is fresh and green. Among the trees we find poplars, willows, pines, and above all the birch with its white stem. Oaks are scarce, and limes and elms need care and culture. The mountain-ash, with its bright red berries, supplies the place of flowering shrubs. Mallows, hollyhocks, and valerians, the melancholy heralds of autumn, even before summer has arrived, give a few glimpses of colour amongst the prevailing green. Everything else is exotic. Indeed the vegetation constantly reminds us that we are much nearer the pole than the equator.

What pleased and surprised me most in the park was a brook, a real German brook, with its crystal clear water rushing over blocks of granite. I could not have believed there was

* Near Potsdam, the residence of Prince Karl.

so great a fall in flat Russia from the Valdai Hills to the sea level.

It is always perfectly unaccountable to me, why landscape gardeners in flat countries will contrive waterfalls instead of turning their attention to the making of, at least for a short distance, a splashing murmuring brook. The artistically tortured water is sent over a plank into a chasm six feet deep, whence it seems to creep away ashamed, not knowing where to go. To make the thing complete, the cataract should only be set off when the spectator is standing in anxious expectation, ready to be astonished!

The brook at Peterhof is natural, and if the trout can ever make a home for itself in the sixtieth degree of north latitude, it must surely find one here.

Higher up the abundance of water has been used to make large lakes, surrounded with trees and very pretty country houses.

In building these every one has followed his own taste. There are Italian villas with the characteristic four-cornered towers, flat roofs, open stairs, terraces and statues; then comes a manor-house in Saxon-Norman style, with heavy gables, projecting balconies, and broad windows, or in the midst of a birch wood, lies a Swiss cottage with its white gable and carved balcony. The greater part of the houses are built of wood, roofed with sheet iron, sometimes painted red, but generally green; and all are constructed more or less for the enjoyment of summer, which, however, does not always come, and this year seems not to be forthcoming at all. The day of our arrival was the only really fine day we have had.

In Russia no one goes out without his cloak, and the climate is such that one quickly learns to follow this rule; for let the weather be bad or good the invaluable cloak protects alike from rain or dust.

Though I was comfortably wrapped up, I had now a mind to return, and called out "domoi" (home) to my Iswoschtschik, who, otherwise would have driven on to Petersburg.

To-day is Saturday, August 16, that is in the dog-days, yet the thermometer hardly rose to fifty-five degrees. Up to this time we have had fires in all the rooms, but as I cannot make up my mind to have my stove lighted, I have put on my winter clothes. General Schreckenstein, who occupies the ground floor, has had his heated. The sky is grey, rain is falling, and there is wind enough to make us congratulate ourselves that we are on land.

The day was passed in visits to the Imperial family, which involved real journeys, for Strelna, where the Grand Duke Constantine lives, is about six miles from Peterhof, in the direction of Petersburg, whilst the palace of Sergmosch, belonging to the Grand Duchess Mary,* lies several miles off in a contrary direction, on the way to Oranienbaum.

As soon as the prince's suite was assembled, accompanied by General Mansouroff and Colonel Mirback, the two Russian officers appointed to attend him, we went first to be presented to the Emperor, who lives in a very simple cottage. The ministers Dolgorouchi, Perofsky, and Schuwalof, came down the little stairs with their portfolios under their arms, and then the Emperor himself appeared.

* Sister of the Emperor of Russia, widow of the Duke of Leuchtenberg.

He made a most pleasant impression on me. He has not the statuesque beauty, nor the marble rigidity of his father, but he is an extremely handsome man of majestic bearing. He appeared somewhat worn, and one could imagine that events had impressed that gravity on his noble features, which contrasts so strongly with the kindly expression of his large eyes. In no country is the person of the monarch of greater importance than in Russia, because nowhere else is his power so unlimited.

On his accession to the throne,[*] Alexander found Europe in arms against him, and he has to carry out reforms in his own vast kingdom, which require a firm hand. It is no wonder that he encounters his tremendous task with seriousness.

The prince presented each of us, and the Emperor knew how to say to every one the right thing with perfect ease. He speaks German and French very fluently, and has an extremely dignified, but at the same time, agreeable manner.

After this we went to Alexandra, a pretty

[*] March 2, 1855.

little country house, in which, notwithstanding its small size, the Emperor Nicolas used to live with all his large family. The children now have establishments of their own, and only the widow and her youngest son* still make it their home. Prince Frederick William is now staying there with his aunt. The Empress-Mother is perfectly charming. "Let each one of them come here to me separately for I cannot see them so far off," said she, as she sat up in her chair to receive us. She gave us her hand to kiss, and had something friendly to say to each. We were received as her dear fellow-countrymen. Before leaving she inquired which of us liked dancing, for she much liked to see cheerful people about her. She laughed and joked and seemed quite pleased.

* Grand Duke Michael, born 1832.

Sunday, August 17.

TO-DAY mass was celebrated in the Pavilion of Peterhof, at which the whole court was present. In the saloons where we assembled I found Severin,* "*Jai vu Madame de Moltke à Berlin, plus belle et plus gracieuse que jamais, et sa belle-mere, qui avait l'air d' être sa soeur.*"

At twelve o'clock the court arrived. The Emperor, who wore a general's uniform—green, with a red collar, ornamented with gold lace— led the way with his aunt, the Grand Duchess of Mecklenburg, who wore a dress of white lace and very beautiful diamonds. On his left hand walked the Empress Marie,† dressed in bright blue with broad point lace.

Then came the four sons of the Emperor, the two eldest in the uniform of the guards, the third in the uniform of the infantry, and the youngest in the blue dress of the navy; after

---

* A distinguished Russian diplomatist, born 1792, died 1865.—Tr.

† Maria Alexandrowna, born 1824, daughter of the late Grand Duke of Hesse, Ludwig II., married to the Emperor in 1841.

them the Grand Duchess Michael — Nicolas, and Prince Peter of Oldenburg and his two sons. All stood during the whole mass, which lasted more than an hour, even the aged Grand Duchess; the reigning Empress alone sat down from time to time.

The chapel is white, richly gilded; the holy of holies, with the altar, is separated from the nave, in all Greek churches, by the Ikonostasis covered with pictures. This has three doors, of which the middle one is called the Emperor's door, the Czar alone having the right of entering it. It is almost always closed, but a kind of lattice-work permits one to see something of what passes behind it.

The Greek Church allows the use of paintings of the saints, and of singing in the service, but forbids all sculpture and instrumental music. They have the most wonderful old hymns, mostly brought from the west, although now forgotten there. Rome has furnished many.

Of course these compositions without instrumental accompaniment are extremely difficult to sing, and require endless practice. The Emperor's choir is now celebrated throughout the world, and I was quite impatient to hear it.

It is composed of about thirty voices, from a bass which makes the windows shake, to the softest soprano of children. The choristers are ranged near the Ikonostasis, and are dressed in crimson frocks and trousers, ornamented with gold lace; and wear swords.

The first part of the service consists of prayers, and in the course of these is repeated in various manners, sung by many voices, "Gospodi Pomilui—*Lord have mercy upon us.*" The priests, in green satin robes embroidered with gold crosses, hold up an enormously big Evangelium ornamented with gold and precious stones.

Baratof, the confessor of the late Emperor, said mass. He had a bass voice, of really incredible depth. The front of his head was close shaven, but behind the hair hung half way down his back. He went about incensing, making the sign of the cross, and saying prayers. When the second part of the mass began, the bread and wine was lifted high above their heads, and the priests retired behind the middle door, and whilst the transubstantiation, the turning of the bread and wine into flesh and blood, was going on, the choir sang a truly overpowering melody with the most perfect execution. Nothing can be heard more beautiful than the composition, but nothing also more beautiful than the rendering. To my great despair an old "Excellency" was standing just behind me, who joined in with the choir, of course considerably out of time; it is true that he sang *sotto voce*, but quite loud enough to spoil my enjoyment. The third part of the service consisted of the administration of the consecrated bread, to which the Imperial family alone remained.

After mass we were presented to the reigning Empress. She has a tall slender figure, and a pleasant expression.

Then we paid our respects to the Grand Duchess of Weimar,* and afterwards began our series of visits. In order to get through my task, I gave the list to the groom, and made him go on first in his droschke, while we all

* Sophia Louisa, born 1824, a Netherland princess. Her mother, Anna Paulina, wife of William II., King of the Netherlands, was sister of the Emperor Nicolas I.

scampered after him, so that we got through twenty-six visits in the course of an hour.

At four o'clock the Emperor gave a grand dinner in honour of the French ambassador, Count Morny, who had brought to the Emperor the ribbon of the Legion of Honour. The Empress-Mother was also present at the dinner. She wore a white muslin dress and a jacket of the same material, trimmed with blue ribbon, about an inch wide, without any other ornament, and a white cap with white feathers, which looked extremely well. The tall, slender figure of the Empress made her look, at a distance, like a young lady.

I sat at table next to Severin. After dinner we were presented to the other Grand Duchesses. The Grand Duchess Marie still looks very well. She wore a rose-coloured dress of Moiré, with a green trimming of long pendulous stalks of grass. But the wife of the Grand Duke Constantine, born princess of Altenburg, is dazzlingly beautiful. She has a tall, elegant figure, a lovely face, and dark brown hair. She wore dark blue and white.

After dinner I walked through the English

garden towards Mont Plaisir, a little pleasure-house close by the sea, which was built by Peter the Great. The situation is very pretty. There are many fine shady trees, and it commands a view of Petersburg. But without sun or warmth there can be no poetry in any landscape.

We were to drink tea here, but I slipped away, in order to write my letter in peace.

The cooking is particularly good, and I wish I could secretly direct Henry to eat of all that is brought to me. At half-past eight o'clock they bring my coffee, which is here always taken in glasses, and no end of excellent pastry. At twelve o'clock they serve for me four different dishes, a bottle of red wine, and a small one of liqueur. Of this I only eat a crust of bread, with a little caviar, and half a glass of wine. The rest disappears in some other way. At four o'clock we have an excellent dinner. At eight I have tea in my room, and yet, after all, up comes the wretch of a footman, and inquires when I will have supper. They carry off the wax lights, when they have hardly burned at all; servants are much the same everywhere.

Monday, August 18.

THIS morning we made an excursion, driving in carriages round the neighbourhood. The Emperor Nicolas has done a great deal for Peterhof. First, he had forty miles of roads made in all directions, then he had great basins excavated for water, which are not only beautiful, but which have in some measure dried the soil, and lastly, on the most beautiful points, he had very pretty villas built. One of these villas, named Oserki, much resembles Charlottenhof, near Potsdam.

One of the most important buildings is Babigon, on the top of a hill, from which there is an extensive view over land and sea as far as Petersburg and Cronstadt. But in truth one does not here wish for an extensive view. The land, whenever one leaves the park roads, is wet, spongy marshland, with low brushwood here and there. The sea is grey and monotonous, at any rate under the gloomy sky we have to-day.

The pavilion itself is splendid, entirely built of granite, marble, and sandstone. On a basement of granite blocks somewhat in the Egyptian style, two storeys are built, each surrounded with pillars, the monoliths made of fine dark granite cut and beautifully polished. The capitals of white marble are in the lower storey Corinthian, in the upper Doric, which is indeed unusual, though not more than an Attic Temple in two storeys. In front of this building stand the famous statues of the two horse-tamers by Baron Klodt, which we have also in Berlin, and which the popular wit has baptized by the name *gehemmten Fortschritt und den beförderten Rückschritt* (arrested progress, and advanced retreat). The whole is built with a solidity unusual in Russia, as if for eternity. It makes a very pleasing impression.

In the afternoon the Prince took us for a walk in the opposite direction, that is, towards Oranienbaum. The road which leads to it is wonderfully beautiful. On the left lies a chain of low hills, with an unbroken series of villas and gardens almost like the road from Altona to Blankenese. Among these the villa of the Grand Duchess Marie, called Sergiewsk, is most remarkable.

Oranienbaum was originally the residence of Admiral Mentschikoff, but belongs now to the Grand Duchess Helen,* who, however, is not residing there at present. The grounds which surround the palace are very much like those of Peterhof. The principal building is white and yellow, and is surmounted by a kind of cupola, which supports a crown quite twenty feet high. Two pavilions are joined to the main building by galleries. In front is a long terrace, from which the descent is made by fine granite steps. Here also is a canal to the sea, but the fountains are wanting. On the other hand, the view is much richer here than at Peterhof, for Cronstadt, with its cupolas, its fortified islands, and its forest of masts, makes a most picturesque background. The surface of the water is so smooth that it reminds me of the Lagunes, and if one could take a very tall and large factory chimney for the tower of St. Mark's, we might imagine we were looking at Venice in her pride. The palace is besides very habitable

* Daughter of Prince Paul of Wurtemburg. Married the Grand Duke Michael. She was born 1807, and died 1873.

and comfortably furnished. Low rooms and narrow windows were formerly used everywhere, and they correspond with the climate. The great panes of plate glass, making us fancy ourselves out of doors, belong to a later and more luxurious age.

Tuesday, August 19.

TO-DAY we went to Cronstadt, the Grand Duke Constantine himself being our guide, which made it excessively interesting and instructive, for, in the first place, he understands the matter, and then he is uncommonly frank. Indeed, there is no mystery made about this fortress. Admiral Napier lately remained there for eight whole days, and they showed him everything. They are right in this, for these imposing tower-like works can easily be seen so well from a distance, and besides they gain by a nearer acquaintance. Much has been said of plastered walls, and of casemates which collapse with the firing of their own guns. How far this may have been true in Sebastopol I do not know. Here I found walls ten feet thick of pure granite, from Lake Onega, which contains less mica than the Finland granite, and is much harder. The vaults were of brick, very well built. The navigable channel in the Bay of Finland becomes ever narrower as it approaches Petersburg. Near the island of Cronstadt it is only about a thousand feet broad, and on both sides of it rise enormous fortifications; on the right Kronslot, and Risbank, and on the left the Alexander, Peter the Great, Mentschikoff, and other smaller forts. They are casemated up to the third storey and above the platforms, and turn to the side of the entrance alone fifty or sixty cannon, each of the heaviest calibre. There lie the immense Paixhan guns, which discharge hollow balls of over a foot in diameter with the greatest precision, making holes which can hardly ever be stopped, and which, if they burst in the middle of a ship, would cause endless devastation.

To reach Petersburg or return from it, between these fortifications, is quite impossible. There are besides, two ships of the line lying across the channel, with floating batteries between them.

However imposing these high, gigantic fortresses look, it would undoubtedly have been better to place the same number of guns on low batteries; but some of the buildings were already there. There was a very extended line to defend. The work would have been extraordinarily laborious and costly, as the foundations must have been laid in a shifting soil, at the depth of nineteen feet of water. Of course the high, broad walls present an unfailing aim to the guns of a ship, and it is a question whether it may not be possible to make a breach in them from a great distance. The Grand Duke Constantine had fired against Risbank with very heavy shot from a small distance (three hundred yards). The long six-and-thirty pound gun penetrated the farthest, but not more than eight inches. The ball fell in splinters. Clearly, one must fire a long time before even one part of the fortifications could be made useless. The Russians, too, have not failed to make use of their experience at Sweaborg. I found a great number of sixty pound guns of such a strength of metal, that they can carry a charge of eighteen to twenty pounds of powder, and have the enormous range of over four versts, or more than three miles.

In earlier times they attempted to make it impossible for vessels of even small draught to get round the fortress, by sinking a row of blocks of stone to within three feet of the surface of the water, between Cronstadt and the coast of Finland. But these lines were laid too far back, and it was possible, in spite of them, to bombard the city by means of flat-bottomed vessels. The Russians, therefore, have not shunned the labour of laying down a new line in advance of the other, and have even carried it on also in a southerly direction towards Oranienbaum, on the Ingermanland coast. This long barrier extends for more than twelve miles, and is, for the breadth of a verst (about a mile) barricaded with posts, so that no vessel, even the smallest, can pass through. A landing on the west point of the island itself could only be effected under the fire of the great forts, and the enemy would then be met by two lines of field works, and lastly by the exceedingly strong casemated front of the fortress of Cronstadt.

When the united efforts of the greatest maritime powers, by enormous sacrifices, destroyed Sebastopol, Russia felt it bitterly, but more in a moral than in a material respect. But it would be a deadly blow if a fleet should pass Cronstadt and burn Petersburg. Enormous wealth, and the whole commerce of the country, would be destroyed, and it is conceivable that the seat of government might be once more transferred to Moscow. No efforts to obviate this danger can be too costly.

PETERSBURG, *Wednesday, August* 20.

IT was a very cold, windy, rainy day, and our steamboat took two hours to reach the mouth of the Neva, passing between the countless black and white barrels which mark out the narrow winding channel. The east wind had driven back the water out of the Bay of Finland, so that to the right and left great sandbanks and reaches of mud were visible. There is nothing beautiful in the entrance to the great river until one approaches the Isaak Bridge, where the steam-boat stops, and whence, entering the carriages which await us there, we drove through the finest part of the city across the Admiralty place to the Winter Palace, along the English quays, to the so-called Franzuski Dwor, which is set apart for the reception of the prince and his suite.

That the first sight of Petersburg fell far below my somewhat high-flown expectations might well be caused by the dreadful weather. When laying the foundations of the city, a perfect superfluity of space was found, so that they went to work with the greatest prodigality.

Indeed at that time it was a happy thing when any one could be found who would build houses on these miserable marshes, where afterwards, in the great thoroughfares or near the court, they fetched enormous prices. The squares and streets were all marked out and planned of the most gigantic dimensions; the city was to grow into them. The streets are twice as wide as those in Berlin; they therefore appear empty, and although the houses are mostly of three storeys, they have the appearance of being low. This would not be remedied, even if another storey were added to each house, which is never likely to be done, because there is such an unlimited power of extension in length and breadth. Another consequence of the width of the streets is that they are badly lighted and paved. The swampy condition of the subsoil gives no firm hold to the paving-stones, and therefore, even in the most important parts of the city, the pavement is as bad as it is in the smallest provincial towns of other countries. This gives the city a most deserted appearance, but no one troubles himself about it; because for more than half the year winter paves

Letters from Russia.

the streets in first-rate style. Besides, here, everyone drives; as many droschkies as men are to be seen in the streets. According to statistical accounts, there is in Petersburg one horse to every eight men, which certainly cannot be said of any other great city in the world. People only walk on the broad pathways of Newski Prospect and on the quays, which are made of granite.

And lastly, the building material does not strike me as good, for although in the remote parts of the city many a house is built of wood, yet brickwork is very generally used. The Russians have a predilection for balconies, and above all for columns—both of which are quite absurd in this horrible climate. A round column of brickwork rubbed over with lime is in itself an unhappy idea. The frequent damp places on the houses show how constant is the necessity for repair. The windows are narrow, and next to attic colonnades and low-pitched roofs come buildings in the purest barrack style.

On this sombre canvas I will now touch up my picture with the bright colours for which there is here warrant enough.

Before the Prince alighted at his hotel he went to the Imperial burial-place in Paul's fortress, to visit the grave of his uncle, the Emperor Nicolas, and meanwhile I took the opportunity of settling myself in my rooms, which, being at some height, enjoy a beautiful view over the Neva and its islands. Sunshine and a background alone are wanting. After breakfast we drove to the Isaak Church, of which we had already seen the rich gilded cupola from Peterhof and Cronstadt. This is indeed a splendid edifice. In contrast with all that I have just described, this church is built of the most solid and costly materials which can be found in the whole world, not excepting Rome and Egypt, namely, of granite, marble, and brass.

The Isaak Church is placed in the finest and most open space of the city, and whole forests of piles are rammed into the ground, in order to make a firm foundation for it. Great blocks of granite follow, till the platform is reached on which the church is built. The form of the ground-plan is a cross, whose arms from east to west are twice as long as those from south to north, where the principal entrance is placed. The altar is in the long eastern arm, and is separated from the rest of the church by the Ikonostasis.

The entrances on the north and south are formed by two peristyles on pillars, which exactly resemble those of the Pantheon, and certainly are not of smaller size; for these pillars are fifty-six feet high, seven feet in diameter, and each made out of one single block of granite. They are the same size as the famous pillars at Baalbec in Syria, only those are made in three pieces, whilst the Finland marshes have supplied such unbroken masses of rock as are only found elsewhere in upper Egypt. I have seen something of the same kind in the church of *Sta Maria degli Angeli*, where the four pillars were brought from the baths of Diocletian. Enormous doors of the same material, sculptured most beautifully, lead into the interior of the church, where the whole arrangement brings St. Peter's to mind. There are the same great square pillars which support the dome, but here the dome is only sixty feet in diameter, whilst that of the Pantheon, St. Peter's, the cathedral at Florence, St. Sophia, and even of St. Paul's in London, are more than double the width. For this reason the interior of Isaak's Church does not make the overwhelmingly beautiful impression which is made by the Pantheon, where at a glance is seen two thousand square feet of space roofed over by a single vault. The byzantine domes are all narrow and high, often like towers, as in the Mainz Cathedral, and that of the Isaak Church has besides on the outside four-and-twenty columns, like the dome of the Johannes Church in Potsdam. These pillars are also of granite with bronze capitals, and therefore the richly gilded roof appears like a semi-circle instead of the segment of a circle. The whole is surmounted by the lantern, which is also gilded, and is the repetition, in a small size, of the dome; while on the summit is placed a cross. The interior is only lighted by the windows in the dome, thus producing the mystic twilight desired in Russian churches, which, however, prevents appreciation of the great splendour and richness of the materials employed. In the Ikonostasis there are, near the Emperor's door, two colossal pillars entirely of *lapis lazuli*, then six of the same size, of malachite. Of course the outside only is covered with these precious marbles, which are never found in large pieces. Between these pillars are pictures of the saints; several of them in mosaic, as in Rome. The pavement and all the walls are covered with the most beautiful designs, executed in the finest marble and porphyry. It is inconceivably grand, and the whole building a marvel of splendour. The height of the cupola is more than three hundred feet, to the top of the cross three hundred and forty feet, or about the height of the spire of Magdeburg.

With the Russian Greek form of Church nothing grander could possibly be attained. She has debarred herself from the brighter splendour the Roman Catholic Church received from heathen antiquity, as well as from the long naves and heavenward pointing towers of the German style. The absolute necessity of shutting off the Holy of Holies by the Ikonostasis hinders a clear view of the whole. The heavy pillars take up a very great space, and do not seem to be required by the small side pressure of the narrow cupola.

All that can be done under these circumstances has been done in the Isaak Church, and no one can leave it without admiration. For myself two things in it disturb me. Sculpture is in general so strictly excluded that even the carved work on the great bronze doors is an exception. But here, between the windows and the cupola, there stand colossal figures of angels, made of brass and gilded, which to my feelings make the whole look more confined and smaller than it really is. Through the Emperor's door in the Ikonostasis, may be seen the window behind, which is filled in with a Christ in painted glass. This work of art is from Munich, and is in itself wonderfully beautiful; but the colours of the glass-painting are so intense that they are not in harmony with the paler colouring of the cupola, but rather kill it. If the church were lighted by side windows, it might perhaps be more harmonious. But in the faint twilight of the cupola, which makes even *lapis lazuli* and malachite look pale, the glass-painting seems too bright.

The whole of this immense and magnificent edifice was made by the Emperor Nicolas, who has done more than all his predecessors for the beautifying of Petersburg. He did not see it finished: indeed, they are still at work on the interior.

I drove with the Prince to Kamennoi Ostrow, to pay a visit to the Grand Duchess Helena, a lovely and pleasant lady, and then to dinner with the Grand Duchess of Weimar at the Island of Jelagin. This is a very beautiful Imperial residence on another island, with splendid oak trees and the best turf that I have seen here. Unhappily it rained without ceasing. After dinner we returned to our hotel, and then went for a drive to Newski Prospect. Peter the Great did not take the palace for the middle point of his city, but the high gilded point of the admiralty tower, because it was through the maritime greatness of the city that it was to be united with the continent of Europe. From this point radiate the three chief streets of the city, Newski Prospect, Erbsen Street, and Wosnesensk Street, which runs south and south-east, and the other streets were regulated accordingly.

The Prospect is now the street of fine shops.

The gutter is generally in the middle, and on each side a causeway paved with wood for the innumerable carriages; then come broad pathways in front of the shops, whose magnificence is far famed, but which I found in reality to be quite insignificant. They are not to be compared to those of Paris, London, or Berlin, whether in outward show, or still more particularly, in the value of their contents. We visited the Annitschkoffschen Palace, where the Emperor Nicolas lived before he ascended the throne. It is nothing but an ornamented barrack—white walls with gilding and chandeliers—nothing more.

I afterwards went to see Countess Münster, and then to Severin, whom I did not find at home. It was now nine o'clock, and we took tea with the prince, when Count Redern gave us some music. We played a game of billiards and then went home, thoroughly tired with sightseeing.

Letters from Russia.

Thursday, August 21.

THIS morning the wind blew strongly from the east, and it was very cold, but the sun shone clear and bright, which made the view from my windows very beautiful and lively. The Neva is a fine, majestic, calmly-flowing stream. Its waters collect in Lake Onega, a great basin of a hundred square miles, away from all impurities; they are perfectly clear, but that they are as green as the Rhine water I have not yet been able to discover. That is the case, so far as I have found, only in rivers which flow from chalk hills. The water of the granite formation is quite colourless, and that from slate mountains is grey. Since there is here no want of space, even the merchant vessels do not anchor very close to one another, but at some considerable distance, and it is but seldom that a small steam-vessel passes beyond Isaak's Bridge. Different indeed it looks from the muddy Thames, with its tidal flux and reflux, on which there are just as many steam-vessels as there are here droschkies in the street. The Neva is about as broad as the Rhine at Cologne, but in the city it divides into several branches. People long doubted whether it were possible to make a bridge over the river. The late Emperor accomplished this work also. The Nicolas' or Isaak's Bridge leads from the Platz before the Isaak's Church to the Wasilewskoj Islands, and consists of sixteen stone pillars with arches of iron. It remains to be seen whether it will stand the tremendous pressure of the ice. At one end of this fine bridge, which is about seven hundred feet in length, there is a block of granite thirty-five feet long, twenty feet broad, and fourteen high, on which stands Peter the Great on horseback. He is restraining his horse, which is in full gallop, with both fore-feet in the air. The tail of the animal touches a serpent trodden on by the horse, and is important, as it makes the third support for this colossus, of which the fore-part was made light, while behind it is weighted with lead, in order to preserve its equilibrium. The Emperor stretches out his hand towards the land and sea he had just conquered. The inscription "To Peter the First, Katharine the Second," shows the proud self-assertion of the Empress.

At the other end, but still on the bridge itself, is a chapel to St. Nicolas, very elegantly built, with three of its sides made of glass.

Two hundred years ago no one in Europe knew anything about the Neva. For thousands of years the river had flowed through untrodden forests. No vessel was borne on its bosom, and only the Finland hunters occasionally passed along its banks. Now the Neva is famed throughout the world; it is one of the arteries of the Russian Empire; it carries merchant fleets, and supplies the daily needs of five hundred thousand men. It alone gives clear, pure water, where all the springs are brown and undrinkable; yet the city is constantly in danger from the Neva. The Bay of Finland makes a triangle, of which one of the points is towards Petersburg. A strong west wind drives the tide with great force into this hole or funnel, turning the current so that the Neva flows backwards. Now if this happens at the same time as the breaking up of the ice, the danger is much increased. The islands are first overflowed, next the quays, and then, as the highest point of the city is only fifteen feet above the ordinary level of the sea, all is soon under water. In many parts of the city the water-mark of 1824 is still shown. In several places it rose to the second storey. Many persons were drowned, and the disease caused by the moisture it left behind lasted for a long time. A city whose progress and development had been more historical would never have grown up in such a defenceless situation. But the iron Czar willed it so, and all later generations must accept the consequences.

By nine o'clock we were all in motion to see the Winter Palace. This building is in the form of a square with additional courts, and is about the same size as the Palace at Berlin, but the outside is not nearly so imposing in appearance, although it has one floor more, besides the great cupola. The Winter Palace, with its pillars standing half-way out from the walls, is entirely covered with whitewash, and then coloured over with a dirty brownish-yellow. Near it, and joined to it by arches, is the house of the Empress Catherine, to which she herself gave the name of "the Hermitage," but which is quite as large as the Winter Palace. Including this palace and the French house in which we are living, the Imperial residence has a front along the Neva of eight hundred feet. It is said that six thousand people live in it, and there is even a legend that there are sheep and cows kept under its roofs.

It is well known that the Winter Palace was burned down with all the art treasures it contained, and was rebuilt by the Emperor Nicolas in one year. To accomplish this, the whole space had to be heated during the winter in order to keep the mortar in a fluid state. Then a great hall fell in just as the Emperor had left it. But here also the will of the Empèror sufficed, and the palace was completed at the appointed time. It has a very fine staircase, and is so far magnificent, that it contains an incredible number of very large saloons, one of them two hundred feet long. The interior decoration leaves much to be desired. It is almost all white and gold : often the walls are only whitewashed, and adorned with immense and generally fine pictures of Russian victories.

The apartments, however, in which the Imperial family themselves live on the Neva and

Admiralty Square are extremely pretty and elegant, especially those of the Empress' mother. It seems that her son had endeavoured to bring together everything to make for her here in the north a charming and agreeable residence. The pictures and sculptures are the most costly masterworks of all countries. The view through the well-fitting windows with their great panes of plate-glass, is the pleasantest one can have here, for a winter-garden with splashing fountains encloses the whole of this beautiful suite of rooms.

Above these apartments are those of the Emperor, very comfortable, but without any great beauty. Here are seen many reminiscences of Berlin and of the late king, whom the Emperor highly esteemed. Here hang the great pictures* by Krüger of the Parade at Berlin, the city of Kalisch, and many interesting portraits. Here also was the telegraph by means of which the autocrat's commands were flashed through the wide expanse of his kingdom. A winding

* Franz Krüger, born 1796, died 1857, a German painter celebrated for his portraits of men and horses. —Tr.

staircase leads up from the apartments of the Empress.

Besides this, in another part of the palace, in the north-western corner of it, there is a vaulted room with but one window, which was the favourite chamber of the great Emperor, the ruler of the tenth part of the human race, for whose welfare pray Greek, Catholic, and Protestant Christians, Mohammedans, Jews, and Heathen in the four quarters of the world, in whose territory the sun never sets, and in one part of which for half a year it never rises. Here lived the man whom his people loved and whom Europe hated, because it feared him, though it was compelled to respect him—the man whose personal appearance subdued the wildest uproar of the people; at whose command in the first cholera epidemic, the furious multitude sank on their knees to supplicate the pardon of God, at the same time delivering up their ringleader; the man, lastly, whose will involved Europe in a war which broke his own heart. Here, in this room, he died.

This room has been kept exactly as it was when the Emperor last saw it. The iron camp-bed with the same bedclothes, the coarse Persian shawl, and the cloak with which he covered himself, the various little articles for the toilet, the books and maps of Sebastopol and Cronstadt; everything remains untouched, even the thoroughly worn-out slippers, which he, I believe, wore for twenty-eight years, and always would insist on having mended again. The wall kalendar, which was set daily, stands at the day of his death. The bed stands across the middle of the room, and the last glance of the monarch through the large window fell, perhaps, on the broad, proud Neva, which he had fettered with his bridge, on the golden cupola of his Isaak's Church, and on the sun sinking in the sea behind the fortifications of Cronstadt. Grief at the issue of the war was the disease which killed the Emperor Nicolas. This antique character could not bend his will—he must die.

We went to the Hermitage, which has lately been made into a true temple of art. The greatest treasures of art, the most celebrated master-pieces of painting and sculpture from all countries, twenty thousand gems, a mass of manuscripts, antiques, mosaics, and jewels, are here collected, and these are not exhibited as in other museums, but dispersed among countless rooms and halls, each of which is in itself a beautiful work of art. There is no celebrated painter who is not represented here by one of the finest creations of his genius. Raphael, Correggio, Ruysdael, and Claude Lorraine fill whole rooms, and the Titians seem to me particularly admirable.

There is a very curious collection from the excavations near Kertch in the Crimea, where Greek civilisation flourished four centuries before Christ, till the country was devastated by the Scythians, and then re-peopled by the Golden Horde. There are sarcophagi with golden ornaments of the finest workmanship. Amongst other things they found the skeleton of a man with a golden crown, the mouth of which had all the teeth complete but one. The wife of this man, who apparently had been immolated, was laid by him, and among the ornaments buried with them was found an elegant golden urn, on which was beautifully worked in relief a representation of the husband with a Colchian dentist pulling out a tooth!

I spare you the description of all these wonderful things. It would take many weeks to inspect them.

After luncheon we visited the arsenal and powder manufactory, and towards evening the prince drove back to Peterhof. I shall remain here till we set out for Moscow.

At sunset I went with Prince Hohenzollern up the Admiralty Tower, from whence we had a splendid view over the whole city, and the Neva with its various branches and islands. It only wants a background, the country being perfectly flat. Nothing is to be seen over the enormous mass of houses but a dark strip of sea with countless steamboats sending up columns of smoke. The foreground, however, is bright enough. After tea I shall write again till one o'clock.

Friday, August 22.

THANK God, it is fine once more! though cold and windy.

Just opposite to me, on the other side of the stream, are the high walls and granite battlements of Paul's fortress, which is built on a little separate island. This fortress, being situated quite in the middle of the city, cannot contribute to the defence of Petersburg. But it plays the same part with regard to the Winter Palace as the Castle of St. Angelo does to the Vatican, only here the communication is by water; there by a vaulted passage. The church is in the middle of the fortress, in which all the Emperors of Russia since Peter the Great are entombed, as all Czars before his time were buried in Moscow. The slender mast-like tower rises three hundred feet above the church. It is covered with the gold of ten thousand ducats, but it has become so crooked that it has been surrounded with an enormous scaffolding. Everything in this boggy soil and dreadful climate needs constant repair.

In this fortress is kept the enormous store of

bullion which constitutes the security for the paper-money in circulation. However, I have not counted it. In commerce notes only are seen, rarely silver. Platina is no longer coined; its production has much decreased, and the value of this metal is so uncertain that it cannot serve as a *standard*. Platina is at this moment four times as dear as it has been for twenty years. On the contrary, the yield of gold increases, and hence the enormous wealth of the Government and of some private persons—the Demidoffs for example.

Saturday, August 23.

A RAINY day. In the forenoon I wrote, and then went to *Gostinoy Dwor*, a great two-storied caravanserai, with vaulted passages and vaults in which the shop people lay out their wares and expose them for sale. No one remains here at night; fires are forbidden, only a lamp is lighted under the saint's picture in each cell. The saints themselves attend to these, that no harm may happen.

I bought some leather stamped with gold, and some tea which comes to Russia by land through Siberia to Kiachta. This so-called caravan tea preserves the fine flavour which is always lost in long sea voyages. The price is from three or four silver roubles up to thirty or even fifty roubles a pound. How one tea can be five-and-twenty times as valuable as another, admitted to be good, I know not. At the Court they do not give more than five roubles a pound, and then they mix it with green tea at four roubles.

Afterwards I went to see the new palace of Michaelowski, which, to judge from the exterior, is the most beautiful edifice in Petersburg. It belongs now to the Grand Duchess* Katharine. The interior is not to be seen, as they are putting down new floors.

I then drove on to the old Michaelowski Palace, which the Emperor Paul fortified, when he began to fear his subjects. He lived there only three months. It is now used as the School of Engineers, and they showed me some very fine models, among which those of Sebastopol, Cronstadt, Sweaborg, and Bomarsund, are interesting. The model of Sebastopol shows how this place was to have been fortified. They assure me that at the moment of the advance of the English and French, with forty thousand men after the battle of the Alma, the naval suburb was quite defenceless. Then the garrison only numbered sixteen thousand men, so that there is no doubt that if the allies had known the real state of affairs they might easily have taken the fortress. The great ramparts on the north side too were not at all secure from assault.

I visited in passing the church of Notre-Dame

* Daughter of the Grand Duke Michael, born 1827, married George, Duke of Mecklenburg, Strelitz.

de Kasan, celebrated for its immense treasures of pure silver. The predilection of the Russians for pillars has here been fully gratified; not only have they imitated the great colonnade of St. Peter's at Rome, but also in the interior there are forty granite columns each made of one block. As there is absolutely no space here for these columns, which have nothing to support but the weight of their own capitals, they are placed in two rows, a veritable *embarras de richesse*.

In the evening we visited the imperial library.

It was to-day just such weather as we have in November, and it made me feel quite melancholy.

Sunday, August 24.

OUR expedition to-day was to the School of Mines, where we were shown the mining models, arranged in very fine rooms; some very beautiful minerals, precious stones, and pearls; amongst others the largest nugget of gold which has yet been found, which is worth a hundred and fifty thousand roubles, and a large piece of aqua-marine a foot long and three inches thick, which is worth a still larger sum.

From the School of Mines I drove to a house which was the first that Peter the Great built, when he was laying the foundations of Petersburg, and in which he lived a long time. It is quite a small tenement, with a balcony painted red, and roofed with shingles. The windows are set in lead. A sofa and various utensils which were used by him are shown; and especially the first boat with which the Emperor crossed Lake Ladoga, and which is called the grandfather of the Russian fleet. There is a house built over it in order to preserve it for all time.

Afterwards we went to see the handsome

church of Smolnoi, which is better lighted and more spacious than any of the others. The pictures of the saints are ornamented with diamonds and jewels of great price. Adjoining the church are palatial buildings for the reception of noble ladies. But as the youngest of them is and must be forty years old, we did not linger there, but hastened to see the summer-garden, in which, on May-day, the marriageable Russian girls display themselves, and are reviewed by the candidates for the marriage state, and often carried home at once. The finest thing in this garden is the beautiful iron trellis, which shuts it off from the quay, and a statue of the famous poet Krylow,* on the pedestal of which all the animals of his fables are represented in bronze in the most humorous fashion.

Not quite to lose the power of walking, we now made a promenade to the equestrian statue of Peter the Great, through the Morskoi

---

* A most popular Russian poet, born 1768, died 1844. His fables, full of wit and genius as they are, are simple enough to be used commonly as the first reading-book for children, and many sentences from them have become proverbial expressions.—TR.

and the Neva Prospect. The weather was very fine for walking, but we had only nine degrees of heat, and I had to dress in winter fashion.

To-morrow we are going a hundred miles southwards, yet we shall not get farther south than Memel, the most northerly point of our Fatherland. Still I hope for a somewhat better climate.

Before noon we drove to the celebrated convent Alexander Newski, which, with the many houses and chapels belonging to it, is surrounded with moats and walls, so that it has the appearance of a fortress. This convent is called a *Lawra*, of which there are only three in Russia—the convent of the Trinity in Moscow, the convent of the Grottoes at Kiew, and this one in Petersburg, which, although it holds only the third rank, is the seat of the Metropolitan.

An Archimandrite was himself our guide. They showed us the coffin of the Grand Duke Alexander, who gained a victory over the Swedes on the Neva. The coffin is made of five thousand pounds' worth of silver. Prince Hohenzollern and General Schreckenstein, as good Catholics, kissed the relics.

Then we were taken into a chapel where incredible treasures are gathered together. Bishops' croziers covered with jewels, robes and stoles of gold stuff ornamented with pearls, in short, millions, in the form of jewels.

Lastly, we visited the churchyard, quite full of tombstones, where we saw the tombs of Tolstoi, Samoiloff, Demidoff, Bariatinski, and in fact of all the most wealthy families, for to rest in peace here costs three thousand roubles. In one corner lies a simple stone with the inscription "Here lies Suwaroff," which Prince Italijski had placed there. It was, indeed, not necessary to add a word more.

From Saint Alexander's we drove a long way round the town, past the barracks of the Cossacks of the line, to the only convent of nuns which there is in Petersburg, but I do not know its name. It contains, including the novices, a hundred and twenty-five young girls, who submit to a very strict discipline, and never leave the convent.

The "Igumena," or abbess, received us herself very graciously; men were excluded from the service, but the nuns sang at the entrance.

Among these poor creatures, entirely clothed in black, some were aged, almost all ugly, with Tartar features, though now and then with beautiful eyes. The novices wear a pointed, the nuns a cylindrical, black hood, a black veil, and long black garments. One of them directed the choir with a little black stick. It is impossible to describe the exquisite beauty of the singing. There were most beautiful voices, and among them some so deep that one might take them for men's. I have never heard anything so lovely as these old church melodies.

The nuns receive twenty paper roubles yearly —less than a maid-servant gets with us. Everything else they must earn by the work of their own hands. They work with the needle and paint, and the church contains many beautiful specimens of their skill.

After breakfast I went with General Schreckenstein to pay visits to Count Liewen and Prince Gortschakoff, and then once more to the Isaak's Church. The more this church is seen, the more splendid it appears. The colossal size of the bronze reliefs in the gable windows was made very distinct to me. A man who was mending something had put a rope round the neck of the infant Christ, on which he took his unsteady seat. The man appeared only half the size of the infant on his mother's lap. The great pictures of the saints on the Ikonostasis are marvellously beautiful, and are besides all of mosaic. On the left is a Madonna with the infant Christ, nothing more lovely than which can possibly be seen. The fair child in his white shirt stretches out his arms towards the spectator, and in his dark eyes are seen all the gravity and mystery of his great mission. Next to this picture is Alexander Newski in full armour, then St. Katherine; on the right is Christ bearing the globe, St. Isaac Dalmaticus with the ground-plan of the church in his hand, and then another saint. These designs are true masterpieces of art. Between each picture is a column of malachite forty feet high, eight in number. The entrance to the Emperor's door is formed by two priceless columns of *lapis lazuli*, with capitals of gold. The two side-chapels are very beautiful in marble and malachite, white and green. The steps are of *rosso antico*. The floor is made of giallo, porphyry, and a kind of green

Genoese marble, which very much resembles *verde antico*.

After dinner, at seven o'clock, we made a long excursion. Indeed from morning to night six or eight carriages stand ready at the door. It is of no use to attempt to walk here, the distances are so great.

We drove to the islands north of the city, Petrofski, Christofski, Jelagin and Kamennoi Ostrow. The landscape was exceedingly lovely in the light of the setting sun. The banks of the wide branches of the stream are studded with pretty wooden houses and gardens. Dark firs and weeping birches predominate, but on Jelagin there are also very fine oaks. We visited a fine house belonging to Prince Bjeloserski, and the Imperial Palace, and only returned when it was quite dark. The days here are still considerably longer than with us. The view out of my window is also very beautiful at night, when the quays are lighted with gas, and the two bridges which I overlook are lighted with innumerable lamps. But it is twelve o'clock, and I must close. In the morning the Prince will come to the city.

Monday, August 25.

AT a quarter to eleven this morning we started by special train for Moscow. The distance is six hundred and five versts, or three hundred and forty-eight miles, which we accomplished in twenty-two hours, so that the pace is very moderate. The Emperor does it in fourteen hours, or twenty-four miles an hour, which is no great speed; on the Great Western we made forty-eight miles an hour; but they do well not to attempt such performances here, and it is surely a fine thing to be able to travel from one Russian capital to the other in a day; a benefit appreciated in observing the country traversed!

The management of the railway, however, seems to be very good. Along the whole distance there are double lines of rail, the stations are solid and well-built, with even a certain amount of ornamentation : most of them having elegant retiring rooms for the Emperor. The carriages are convenient, but very heavy. The gradients are very slight, as might be expected in this country, being hardly more than 1 in 100, but very long-continued, for the ridge of the Waldai Hills which the railway cuts, is 705 feet high. The railways are made as much as possible in direct lines, without troubling themselves with the fact that, with the exception of the two terminal stations, no town is directly touched by them. Even Novgorod, a town historically famous and still important, is left about eight miles on one side. "*Le chemin de fer fera naître des villes.*" But must the old towns be therefore allowed to perish? *Au reste ils n'ont naquis que des* stations and sleepers. These and the milestones are the only adornments of the desolate country, houseless, flat, and uniform as it becomes as soon as the last suburban houses of Petersburg are left behind. Marshes and alder-bushes as far as the eye can reach, occasionally a few distorted pines, rarely a cultivated field, still more rarely a village. The church with its bright green cupola and white-washed walls makes the villages look well from a distance, but the houses are all miserable wooden sheds, without gardens and without trees.

The villages are not enclosed; no avenues, or farms, or vineyards, or smithies are to be seen.

Letters from Russia.

I am often reminded of the Oberharz, where the little wooden houses are scattered over the meadows as if they had fallen from a sieve. The eye hungers for some undulation of the surface, and therefore the Wolchow stream appears so surpassingly beautiful. It is crossed at a considerable height by a latticed bridge of great length. Large uncouth-looking boats are seen coming from Lake Peipus and Novgorod on this river, which is about as broad as the Elbe, to Lake Onega and so to Petersburg, laden with part of the firewood required by this metropolis.

Still more astonishing in this endless plain is the passage a little farther on of this insignificant stream, which has hollowed out a narrow but very deep valley. It is crossed by a viaduct of quite 1,000 feet long, at the height of at least 120 feet. The enormous pillars are placed on a foundation of brickwork, and then covered with iron plating, apparently because they are carved out of wood. They look like church towers. I think this is very unsafe. We were allowed to observe the bridge from below. The ascent is made by 500 steps. As soon as these two valleys are passed there is the old uniformity again, and only the thought that these little sleepy streams flow on to the Caspian Sea makes them interesting to me.

Call our different repasts what you will, this much is certain, that we have dined three times in due form, and the last time was at nine o'clock in the evening.

General Schreckenstein, Count Redern, Barner, and I, had a coupé between us, and were able to make ourselves very comfortable. And here, I must confess to my shame, that I neither saw Tver nor the Volga, because I was fast asleep.

The next morning, Tuesday, the sun rose beautifully behind the tops of some fir-trees, but the country appeared to be of much the same character as what we saw yesterday, only the trees are better grown, and there are a few really pretty villages; then we came to a fine oak-wood, and suddenly countless towers and cupolas immerged from the plain. We were in Moscow.

I have not yet digested the impression this city has made upon me. I walk about continually in silent astonishment. I try to arrange my thoughts, and to make some comparisons between what strikes me as so strange and wondrous, with what I have seen before in other regions. When I stand on the high terrace of the Kremlin and look down on this enormous city, the white houses with bright green roofs, surrounded with dark trees, the high towers and countless churches with golden cupolas, I am reminded sometimes of the view of Prague from the Hradschin, sometimes of that of Pesth from Buda, and again of that of Palermo from Monte Reale. Still, everything here is different, and the centre of the whole, the Kremlin, cannot be compared to anything in the world. These walls, fifty or sixty feet high, white with pointed battlements, the gigantic gate-towers, the huge palace of the old czars, the residence of the patriarchs, the bell-tower of Juan Weliki, the peculiar old churches, form a whole which is not to be found twice in the world.

The first day was taken up with visits and looking at the vast exterior of the Kremlin. They have set aside three houses for the Prince. But I live quite close to him in the palace of Princess Trubetzkoi, who is absent at present visiting her estates.

Thursday, August 28.

THE city of Moscow assumes that the Emperor has not yet arrived. Some, indeed, assert that he has been staying since yesterday, at the Palace of Petrofskoi, which is some miles from here, in order to hold a court and to review 100,000 of the Guards : but he is there *incognito*; officially he has not arrived.

The holy city is preparing itself for the entry which is to take place to-morrow. In all the streets and open spaces a knocking and hammering is going on. Most of the houses here stand singly in the midst of a garden or courtyard. In these spaces between the houses great platforms are erected for the spectators. On one of them alone I counted three thousand numbered seats. Before the houses too, small stages are erected and filled with chairs—all roofed over with canvas and ornamented with coloured cloths, carpets, and flowers. Seats are thus easily provided for several hundred thousand, by which all inconvenient crowding is prevented. Only those who cannot pay the few copeks, the Tschornoi narod, the "black race," of the people, will form the movable part of the spectators, and the police will be there to keep them in order.

The churches and palaces have thin laths nailed all along their architectural lines, on which to fix the lamps for the illumination. The immense church Iwan, which will speak out with its five-and-twenty great bells, has a crown made of lamps put round its golden cupola, above which blazes the mighty cross, which was pulled down with so much difficulty and danger by the French, and which the Russians triumphantly replaced. As an atonement for this injury a thousand field-pieces taken from the French are laid at the feet of Iwan, where Count Morny may see them to-morrow.

Half the population of the city are walking about the streets, and they are allowed to go everywhere, even into the Kremlin, to see the preparations which are still going on there.

Every day teams of horses are being sent between Petrowskoj and the Kremlin; they are mostly dark grey or black, and are to draw the state carriages of the Empress and Grand Duchesses. The driver sits in a wonderful fashion on the off-leader, and a man also walks on foot by each horse, and leads it by the rein. Yesterday their excellencies bore a frightfully heavy baldaquin on thick staves of gold through the halls and up the steps of the palace. The Emperor's adjutants walked by the side, holding it straight by golden ropes.

The state carriages, wonderful reminiscences of a past age, are brought out of the twilight of the arsenals, where they have stood for eight-and-twenty years. The oldest of them are quite without springs, and are hung by very long straps on to a pole twenty feet long and of great thickness, which is so much bent that the coach almost touches the ground. Those of the Empresses are ornamented with diamonds and jewels. The most ancient can hardly be put in motion. Among others there is a kind of ambulating house of gold, velvet, and crystal, which was given as a present to Peter the Great from England, and compared with the weight of this, a six-and-thirty pounder is mere child's play. In short everything is full of life and animation, in expectation of the roar of artillery which in the morning will proclaim from the ancient gate-towers of the Kremlin the entrance of the Czar.

Yesterday the Emperor rode through the camp of the guards, whom he has not seen since he ascended the throne, because they were away at the war in Lithuania and Poland, and they have now pitched their tents in a wide open plain close by the city. First of all there was a solemn mass, at which the Empress also was present. We drove to the camp in grand style, amid thick clouds of dust, while the Emperor and his suite rode. He looks particularly well on horseback. At this moment it began to rain, and came down in torrents. Happily we were able to take shelter under the tent in which the altar was placed, and where mass was read or rather sung. All further continuation of the fête was countermanded, and we returned home.

In the evening I drove to Petrowskoj. It lies in the midst of woods, and has a very strange appearance. The palace itself is a square building of two storys, with a green cupola. The entrances are supported by most peculiar bottle-shaped pillars, and the whole is surrounded by turreted walls, with battlements and loop-holes. This red and white striped fortress, from which the light streamed through high windows out into the dark woods, seemed like a scene in a fairy tale of the thousand and one nights. Here all convents and palaces are fortified. They were the only tenable spots when the Yellow Hordes with twenty or thirty thousand horses rushed through this flat country, and devastated it completely. Long after their yoke was broken, the Tartars of the Khanate of the Crimea were still a formidable enemy. There used to be watchmen constantly on the highest battlements of the Kremlin, looking out over the great plain stretching away to the south; and when they saw clouds of dust whirling up, the great bell (Kolokol) of Iwan Weliki sounded out the call of distress, and everyone fled for shelter to the palace of the Czar or the convents, at whose walls the troops of furious horsemen knocked and hammered in vain. The Christianity, the learning, and the civilisation of the Russian people, all took refuge in the convents, and it was from the convents that deliverance from the yoke of the Mongolians and Poles came at last.

To-day mass was said in the open air, and five battalions received new colours, which had been consecrated for this purpose. Then the Metropolitan passed along the front and sprinkled the troops vigorously with holy water, so vigorously that some even dripped with it. The Emperor and the two Empresses kissed not only the cross, but the priest's hand. Then the Emperor hastened to place himself in front of the battalion, and spoke some words to the men in military fashion, which were answered by endless cheering. He sat a well-trained horse very well; afterwards he rode along the whole length of the camp one and a half (German) miles. Seventy-four battalions, eight hundred strong, about sixty thousand men, tall and strong, bearded, with dark brown faces, stood unarmed, and with caps uplifted.

I will say nothing of the deafening hurrahs which lasted for two hours, but I could see how delighted these bearded men were to see their Czar.

The Emperor spoke to several of them, who replied to their "Batuschka" (Father) without any embarrassment. In Russia the family is the microcosm of the State. All power rests upon paternal authority. All theories of representative government are, in Russia, simple nonsense. "How can human decrees limit the divine right of a father?" says the Russian; and indeed the unlimited power of the Emperor is a necessity and a benefit in a country where nothing is done if it is not commanded by a superior.

Any one who stands, as I did, on the top of the Kremlin, and looks down for the first time on the city of Moscow on a warm sunny day, will with difficulty realise that he is in the same latitude under which in Siberia the reindeer roams, and in Kamschatka dogs draw sledges over fields of ice. Moscow makes a most decidedly southern impression, though at the same time something strange and novel. I fancied myself in Ispahan, Bagdad, or some place in the *Arabian Nights*.

Although Moscow does not contain more than 300,000 inhabitants, yet with its gardens, houses, churches, and convents, it covers the space of two square German miles. In this flat country there is scarce any view beyond the farthest suburbs, and houses and trees stretch as far as the horizon.

No city in the world, not even excepting Rome, contains so many churches as the holy Stolitza of Russia. They say that Moscow has forty times forty houses of God. Each of these has five, some even as many as sixteen cupolas, which are gaily painted and roofed with coloured glazed tiles, or richly silvered and gilded, so that they shine and glitter against the blue sky like the sun when it has but half risen above the horizon. Even the slender towers, which here and there rise above the enormous mass of houses and gardens to a considerable height, are decked with this sparkling covering, and the finest palaces are never without a cupola.

The houses are almost always surrounded with gardens, and their flat roofs of bright green or red and their white walls, stand out in very marked outlines on the back-ground of dark trees. Only the Chinese quarter, the oldest part, close to the Kremlin, called Kitai-gorod, forms anything like what we call a town, where house joins to house, and this is carefully enclosed with a finely-turreted wall, and of course painted white. All the rest of the city has the appearance of a collection of country houses, between which the Moskwa flows in great curves.

On the hill of the Kremlin, close to the palaces of the Czar and the patriarchs, are the arsenal of the army and the sacred places of the church. There are enthroned the highest secular and the highest spiritual power. The convents, which are mostly in the outer parts of the city, are fortresses in themselves.

The merchants, the *Kupzi*, settled themselves in Kitai-gorod, in order to protect behind its walls the treasures they brought from China, Bucharest, Byzantium, and Novgorod. All else, and by far the largest part of the city, was built by the nobility, and long after the first Emperor had erected a new capital on the enemy's territory, these, the magnates of the kingdom who still clung to the customs of their fathers, disdained the new city.

And the venerable Moscow with its ancient sanctuaries, relics, and historical reminiscences is still for every Russian an object of reverence and love, and as soon as he, even from the distance of a hundred miles, catches sight of the golden cross on the church of Ivan Weliki, he falls on his knees with devotion and patriotism. Petersburg is his pride, but Moscow lies next his heart.

Moscow has really no resemblance whatever to Petersburg. Here there is no Neva, no sea and no steamboats, no regular street, no great squares, no wooded islands. But as little does Moscow resemble any other city. The cupolas, flat roofs, and trees, might remind us of the east, but in the east the cupolas have flat arches, are roofed with grey lead, and topped with slender minarets; in the houses there are no windows looking out on to the streets, and the gardens are enclosed in monotonous, high walls. Moscow has a character all its own, and if it must be compared with anything, we can only call it Byzantine-moorish.

Russia, indeed, received her Christianity and her first civilisation from Byzantium. She has been till quite recent times, absolutely without communication with the west, and therefore developed the elements of civilisation given her by the east in a manner perfectly national.

The yoke of the Monguls and Tartars which lasted three hundred years, long hindered all further progress. Civilisation was quite confined to the convents, and it was from the convents that freedom came at last. The Tartar khans never demanded that the vanquished foe should embrace Islamism; they contented themselves with receiving the tribute-money, and in order to raise it, authority within the country itself was required. They therefore strengthened the respect with which the great princes and the clergy were surrounded, and however hardly the domination of these hordes pressed on the development of the country, they nevertheless encouraged among the oppressed people faith in their religion, fidelity to their rulers, and love for their common fatherland.

These characteristics distinguish the Russian people even to the present day; and when we reflect that the essence of this people, the great Russian nation, thirty-six millions of men of one race, one creed, one tongue, forms the greatest homogeneous mass of men in the world, who can doubt that Russia has a great future before her?

It has been said that with increasing population, the enormous kingdom must fall to pieces of itself; but no part can exist without the other, the wooded north needs the corn-growing south; the industrial midland needs them both; while the interior is nothing without the sea-coasts and nothing without the great waterways of the Volga, which is navigable for 1,600 miles. But still more powerful than all these is the community of feeling which binds together even the most distant part.

And of this feeling, Moscow is the centre point, not only in the European empire, but in the old sacred realm of the Czars, in which the historical memories of the people are rooted, and out of which its future may yet perhaps arise.

The foreign civilisation, imposed by force, never penetrated the mass of the people. The national peculiarities have been thoroughly maintained in the language, manners, and customs, as well as in a most remarkable communal constitution, the most free, the most independent that ever existed, and lastly, even in their architecture.

With regard to this, however, it is only a question of the churches. In Russia nearly everything is new. Here, whatever is over a hundred years old is considered to belong to antiquity. The Russian dwelling-house is made of wood, and consequently does not last so long, unless it is protected, like that of Peter the Great, by one of stone placed over it. The Emperor's palaces too are new, and in Moscow only are there still some remains of the old Dworez of the Czars. Churches of the fourteenth and fifteenth centuries exist, a very great age for Russia, and the strongly conservative spirit of the priesthood has caused all the later buildings to be made similar to these.

St. Sophia at Constantinople is the model after which all Russian churches are built. It has been imitated everywhere, but equalled nowhere, not even by St. Mark's at Venice. The material as well as the skill was wanting to vault with one arch a breadth of a hundred and twenty-six feet: therefore what could not be obtained in width was sought in height, and the cupolas were made narrow and high like towers. The unhewn stone, joined without art, required exceedingly strong pillars and thick walls, in which the windows were cut small and deep like loopholes. The brightest light comes through the windows in the thinner walls which support the cupola. Most of the churches are higher than they are long or broad. The thick square pillars contract the space, already small. No clear view is to be obtained, and a mysterious darkness reigns over the whole. The most famous Russian churches have only the tenth part of the height of a Gothic cathedral. Most of them were built, it is true, by Italian masters, but they were obliged to follow the established rule as to form.

As the architectural proportions did not make a grand whole possible, they strove after beauty in the decoration of details and in brilliancy and splendour. Not satisfied with gilding the churches inside and outside, they paved the floors with stones, more or less precious, and ornamented the pictures, which were in themselves of no artistic value, with jewels, diamonds, and pearls. Only the face and hands show the painting; the garments, the crown, and everything else, is covered with gold and silver plating, and jewels.

Sculpture is quite excluded as far as the human figure is concerned, but in painting they do not hesitate to represent God himself. The gold ground which is used so much, is very unfavourable for the flesh tints of the picture, and they have besides the long-drawn contours of the Byzantine and old German schools, without the intensity of expression of the last. Gigantic and frightful pictures often look down from the cupola, which are meant to represent Mary, Christ, John, or God the Father. The Russian buys no pictures of saints which are not either quite black or faded away. A lovely Madonna by Raphael, or a fine Sebastian by Correggio, seems to him not genuine. His faith requires the gloom of his church and the clouds of incense which at every mass veil the mysterious functions of the priest.

The Byzantine element in Russian architecture is also historically easy to explain; the Moorish element arose from the necessity for the ornamentation of individual parts, and only concerns itself with these.

The trellises of the Ikonostasis are interwoven with leaves, bunches of grapes, and the figures of animals : the smooth walls, that is where they are not gilded, display leaf-work, rosettes, or vine-tendrils. Where this is not hewn out of stone it is painted, and where these sorts of designs were impracticable, they called to their aid a variety of the brightest colours. But they are far behind the tasteful, artistic arabesques of the Alhambra, and of the Alcazar.

The most absurd thing I have ever seen in architecture is the Iwan Blajennoj, a church on the square in front of the Kremlin. It is really impossible to describe it. First of all, this building stands on quite uneven ground, although the beautiful smooth square lies straight before it. It is as if it clung to the precipice with its leg hanging down behind it. There is not one trace of symmetry in the whole of it. It has no centre, and no one part is like another. One cupola looks like an onion, another like a pine-apple, an artichoke, a melon, or a Turkish turban. It contains nine separate churches, each with its altar, Ikonostasis, and shrine. In one of them you walk on even ground, in another you go up several steps. Then there is a perfect labyrinth of passages—

some hardly broad enough for two men to pass each other. Of course all these churches are very small, and the one under the principal tower holds hardly more than twenty or thirty people, and yet the roof of it reaches quite up to the top of the tower, so that it is over a hundred feet high. This church is painted inside and out with all the colours of the rainbow, and silvered and gilded. The cupola glistens with red, green, and blue glazed tiles, and the painter has even illuminated the work of the stonemason with colours.

This monstrosity sprang from the head of the monster Iwan Grosnoj—John the Terrible. It is said that when he saw his plan really executed by the skill of the architect, he was enchanted, loaded him with praise, embraced him, and then ordered his eyes to be put out in order to prevent him from making elsewhere a similar masterpiece.

Yet, monstrous as it is, this church does not make an unpleasing impression. Its originality cannot at any rate be denied.

In contrast with this, everything that remains of the old Dworez of the Czars is really beautiful. It is a simple building of four storys, which are each narrower than the one below it, thus leaving a terrace open all round each story. Besides the little house-chapel, which is of extraordinary richness, the second story contains the banqueting-hall, which is built like the Chapter House in Marienburg, only there the whole roof is borne by one slender column, while here the pillar is much thicker. The entrance door is in one corner; the throne stands diagonally in the opposite corner. The walls are now hung with splendid tapestry, and the great throne with cloth-of-gold, which is edged with the finest ermine. These hangings cost forty thousand roubles. The elegant little rooms on the third story are quite charming. The fourth story contains only one large room, which was the Terima, the women's apartment, and in it Peter I. grew up.

There was now an extremely pretty sight: the commanding officers of all the regiments assembled, those of the cavalry regiments being on horseback, to receive the counter-sign, so that we saw a sample of every one of these brilliant uniforms. The cuirassiers with the

Byzantine double eagle on the helmet, like our *Gardes du corps*, but carrying lances; the Uhlans exactly like ours; the hussars in white dolmans with gold lace; the line Cossacks with fur caps and red caftans; the Tschernamorskischen Cossacks in dark blue coats with red scarves; the Ural Cossacks bright blue, all with lances, on little horses with very high saddles. The Tartars are generally heathens or Mussulmen. The Tcherkesses appeared in helmets and coats-of-mail. They went through their extraordinary performances in riding, shooting from horseback with their long guns, protecting themselves against their pursuers with the kantschu, at one time bending down on one side till they could touch the ground with their hands, while at others they stood upright in their saddles. All this at full gallop and accompanied with loud cries.

One regiment particularly pleased me, that of the Drushines, which is raised on the Imperial estates. They wear a cap with the St. Andrew's cross, bare neck, the caftan of the country people, but without buttons, very wide trousers (the shirt outside, like all common Russians), the legs of the trousers tucked into the half-high boots.

Letters from Russia.

This is the uniform of the Mushiks, and is a national, becoming, and practical dress. The man can wear his fur (which is here indispensable) underneath, and I think I may predict that the whole Russian infantry will adopt a similar uniform. *Les proverbes sont l'esprit des peuples,* and the national dress is the result of the experience of centuries, as to what is suitable to the purpose, as well as becoming. The Austrian uniform is white in Moravia, but brown in Banat, according to the colour of the sheep in those countries. The Spaniard wears the tabarra, the colour of the goats which furnish the material of which they are made; the Arab is white from head to foot, because the heat of his climate requires it; and the caftan of the Mushik is adopted not by chance or from caprice, but because it is the best adapted to those who wear it.

The *cortège* of the emperor is really imposing —quite five hundred horses.

I only wish I had a better memory for persons and names. I have come to know a number of interesting men,—that is to say, I have been introduced to them. Prince Gortschakoff,

Lüders, Berg, and Osten-Sacken, who all had commands in the late war; Orloff, Mentschikoff, Adlerberg, Liewen, the Governor of Siberia, and the commander of the army from Caucasus, a host of officers, and the foreign princes and their suites.

It is generally possible to feel happy enough on a strange horse if we are tolerably confident of getting off again without mischief to ourselves or others. But here bad riders come up close behind—horses turn up in the most unexpected corners, plunging and kicking in every direction. It is easy enough to ride alone, but in such a crowd, at a sharp trot on a spirited animal, it is indeed necessary to keep the eyes open. Suddenly the Emperor stops, and all pull up; or he takes a turn, and then the confusion is fearful; or he gallops on, and everyone starts forward, while his head jerks backward with the sudden movement. Then the fluttering flags, the braying of the trumpets, the rolling of the drums, and the never-ceasing "Hurrahs" prepare us to see something. I rode a small black horse which I should have liked for my own: he went just like an East-Prussian, only very eager, taking me more than once in front between the grand-dukes. However, I soon got on very well with him, especially after we came to understand one another. He liked an easy seat and light hand, which in such difficulties was not always possible to give him.

This evening at sunset I went again to the Kremlin. "*Diem perdidi!*" I shall say of every day during my stay here on which I do not visit this wonderful place!

Then I went down to the Moskwa again, and from the very beautiful quay I had a view from below the great white walls, the towers and gates which surround the palace of the czars, and a whole city of churches of the most extraordinary style of architecture. This evening there is to be a great festival in the city, from which I shall excuse myself in order to write. I received so many impressions that it is hardly possible to work out and arrange all my thoughts.

I try to arrive at some understanding of the buildings in this place. In Culm, in West Prussia, I saw last year in the market-place such a peculiar *Rathhaus* that I have never been able to get it out of my head—now I comprehend that it is built after the Moscow style of architecture. There were many relations between the Livonian knights and the German knights in Prussia, and one of their architects may have repeated on the Vistula what he had seen in Moscow. I was reminded here of the East by the fountains, little, round, roofed-over houses in the principal open places, round which men and animals are continually lying, brought there by the necessity for water. At first they seem rude and clumsy when compared with the beautiful architecture, the rich sculpture, the golden lattice-work, and the marble walls of those in the palaces at Constantinople. There are here, just as in the Mosques, enormous flocks of doves, which are so tame that they hardly get out of the way of the carriages and passers by. They are often chased away from the shops like a number of hens, and they are to be seen everywhere picking up their food. No one does them any harm, and to eat them would seem to the Russian a sin. The Gostinoj-Dwor, the market-hall especially, is a reproduction of the oriental Tschurchi; but there the stalls stand farther apart from one another. The little narrow passages which separate them are roofed over; there is the same darkness, and almost the same smell of leather and spices as in the Missir, or the Egyptian market at Constantinople. Here, however, there are almost entirely imported European wares, which can be procured better and cheaper at home, so that there is not much temptation to buy.

If I had to choose, I would much rather live in Moscow than in Petersburg.

Peter the Great found an inland country entirely without sea-coast. He might have chosen either the Black Sea or Baltic to bring him into connection with the civilised world, but whichever it might be, it had first to be conquered. The hot-headed king of Sweden drew him into a northern war, and besides, the southern sea was then surrounded by barbarians. It is said that he had originally intended to found his new capital on the Black Sea, and had even fixed on its site, but the one coast is not much farther from the centre of the kingdom than the other.

What if he had built his Petersburg on the splendid harbour of Sebastopol, never to be blockaded by a winter's ice? or close to the paradise of Tschadyr Dagh, where the vine grows wild, and everything that is found in the conservatories on the Neva flourishes in the open air, where no floods bring destruction, and where the fleet, instead of being frozen up for seven months of the year, might keep up communication with the loveliest lands of Europe more easily than from the Gulf of Finland?

What a city would Petersburg have been, if its wide streets had stretched down to Balaclava, and the Winter Palace had looked on the deep blue mirror of the Euxine; if the Isaac's Church had stood on the heights of Malakoff; if Alushta and Orianda had been the Peterhof and Gatschina of the Imperial family!

Moscow, *August* 29.

THE *entrée joyeuse* which obliges lords and ladies to go in full dress for a mile on horseback or in glass coaches, while half a million of spectators in the streets look on, while the priests in gorgeous vestments bear aloft the sacred vessels and crosses; and a hundred thousand soldiers are to be reviewed—such an *entrée joyeuse* requires of all things the fine sunny day which we have surely a right to expect in the dog-days.

To-day, however, the first day of the festival, began with rain and gloom; but towards noon a bit of blue sky was visible, large enough for a "*pair of marine trousers*," and by and by the weather cleared up and it remained fine, in spite of heavy clouds, till the *entrée* was over.

We were appointed to be at Petrowski by one o'clock, for it takes time to get such a procession into movement. I tried to pass the time of waiting in looking at the monstrous carriages. Thirty of these were drawn by six grays, but that of the Empress by eight dun-coloured horses, all of which were more than six feet high. The Russians drive four or five horses abreast, so they have had a great many coachmen from Prussia who are accustomed to drive four horses from the box, and who here get fifty roubles for doing so. Imprecations in Russian, English, and German were to be heard, as the animals, in spite of all their training, and in spite of the efforts of a footman covered with gold lace at the head of each one, strongly object to move forward with the ponderous vehicles behind them. At last, however, they all moved off.

The harness and trappings are of silk and gold, and the powdered coachman, the pages on horseback, the imperial jägers, the lords in waiting—all are stiff with gold lace and embroidery.

Many more than a hundred generals, and as many imperial adjutants, glittered in stars and ribbons. The troops formed in line from Petrowski quite to the Kremlin; outside the town the cavalry in regiments, and inside the infantry in battalion columns *en ligne*, all dark brown bearded faces. The regiment Paulowsk (in which every man must have a turned up

Tartar nose, because the Emperor Paul was gifted with such a one), wears the pointed metal grenadier cap, such as our first Regiment of Guards wears, and quite a third of the caps showed one or two holes through which bullets had passed.

All the windows and platforms were closely filled, and here the strangest sights were to be seen. Peasants with long beards, merchants' wives literally covered with real pearls, Tscherkessen in their fine national costume, Mingrelian princes who had slings for their head covering, Heathen Tartars, Budhist, Kalmucks, European diplomatists, Mussulman, Swabian peasants, and fine gentlemen from Paris and London.

At three o'clock several cannon shots told that the procession was on its way. First came a division of police in bright blue uniforms, then the scarlet Tscherkesses in coats-of-mail. After these the Marshal in his phaeton, then the Lord Chamberlain in a glass coach and six. Behind these rode two squadrons of cuirassiers with glittering cuirasses, silver eagles on the helmets, and the first armed with lances. Now appeared the Emperor in general's uniform, on a beautiful dapple gray charger, with Prince Friedrich Wilhelm of Prussia on his right; behind him, Prince Friedrich of the Netherlands, the three eldest sons of the Emperor, all the grand-dukes and the foreign princes, then the whole multitude of the different retinues—generals and adjutants. Then came the two Empresses and their ladies in coaches. A division of infantry closed the procession.

Owing to the endless hurrahs of the crowd, the braying of trumpets, the bands of music, the ringing of bells, and the thunder of cannon, many horses were very restive, and every time the Emperor stopped to take the bread and salt from the magistrate, or to be sprinkled with holy water in front of the church, when every one uncovered, the confusion was indescribable.

But everything passed off wonderfully well, and the good order which prevailed in the streets was surprising, although no one hindered the people from seeing their Batuschka, who on his part was never tired of saluting, in a grave but pleasant manner, the people who thronged every window and platform and open space in the city.

As we approached the Kremlin, the guns

thundered from every tower, and the great "*John*" expressed his joy by ringing all the *Kolokols*, which hang around him. Then the great Wetschewoi boomed which had once called the warlike population to arms, in the time of the great Republic of Novgorod, when the Muscovite grand-dukes threatened their freedom, and then there was a booming, and a tinkling, and a humming of all the bells, large and small, far and near, with which Ivan keeps high festival.

Only one bell remains dumb, as in joy or sorrow it has been dumb since the first day of its existence. It stands on a layer of granite, at the foot of the great tower, a house of brass with walls two feet thick. A piece which came out in the casting lies there before it, and leaves a free entrance through which the twenty or thirty men can pass whom this ruined bell can comfortably accommodate.

Before the outer gate of the Kremlin, in a beautiful little chapel, is the image of the Iberian "*Boshja mater*," which is so much venerated that hardly the busiest tradesman passes it by without entering for a moment and crossing himself.

Here the Emperor descended from his horse, and went in to pay his devotions. The whole suite, however, rode through the gate, and marched in front of the wall of the Kremlin on to the great open space, Krasnoj Ploschtschad. The Czar quickly rejoined us, and we all went through the *Redeemer's* door, the sacred *spass woroto*, into the inner court.

Through this door no Russian, and indeed no stranger, passes without uncovering—the highest personage and the lowest alike testify their respect for this miraculous picture of the Saviour. In time past, when the Tartars attacked the Kremlin, such a mist came forth from the picture, that they were unable to find the entrance; and when the French wished to destroy the gate with the arsenal, the tower was cracked all the way down to the crystal plate of the picture, which remained unhurt, and held the whole wall together.

On the other side of the door we dismounted, very well pleased to get out of the crowd of loose horses and stand quietly on the red carpet to await the arrival of the Empresses and the grand duchesses. First came the Empress' mother, and then the reigning Empress in a dress of gold brocade and ermine. The *manteaux* of the grand duchesses were of velvet or lace with gold and pearls. All the ladies of the court wore the national costume, which you know is of scarlet velvet.

Their Majesties now went in solemn procession to Uspenski Sabor, the Church of the Redemption, the veritable cathedral before which the superior clergy awaited the Emperor. This church, in which the coronation takes place, and in which the Patriarchs are buried, is like all Russian churches, extremely rich, but narrow and dark. The great thick pillars take up half the space; the windows are small and deep; the cupolas high and narrow like towers. All the walls and pillars are gilded from top to bottom, and on this gold ground the peculiar, long drawn, often quite distorted, pictures of the saints are painted. Frightful mosaic pictures look down from the cupola above, amongst others one of an old man with a gray beard, which can be no one else but God the Father Himself. I pass over the enormous treasures of gold, silver, and jewels, with which the pictures of the saints are covered, and only notice the book of the gospels of Natalie Narischkin, which was presented by the mother of Peter the Great. The binding is of gold, and is worth a million of roubles. The book has to be carried by two priests, because it is too heavy for one.

The Emperor performed his devotions before the principal images of the saints. He knelt down quite close to me, crossed himself, and kissed the relics. The Empress followed with her long train carried by two pages, and did the same.

The Court of the Redeemer is shut off by a beautiful trellis, and is, except a part of the old palace of the Czars, entirely surrounded by churches, which contain the most sacred relics of Russia. A shorter procession led their Majesties and their whole retinue into Archangelski Sabor, the Church of the Archangel Michael, which contains the graves of all the Czars till the first Emperor, then into Blagowestschenki, or the Church of the Annunciation, which is narrower, more peculiar, and more gorgeous than all the others. It is a perfect little jewel-box. The cross and cupola are of pure gold, and the pavement is inlaid with jasper, agate, and cornelian, from Siberia.

Everywhere the Emperor was received with the wonderful Russian church-melodies, and now that he had given glory to God, the whole splendid procession passed down the open steps, Krasnoi Kryltzo, which were covered with scarlet cloth, to the old Palace of the Czars, which directly communicates with the magnificent rooms of the new palace built by the Emperor Alexander. Then we went through the enormous St. George's Hall, whose walls bear the names of all the knights of St. George, to St. Andrew's Hall, which is like the nave of an old Gothic cathedral, and St. Nicolas' Hall, at the end of which is the throne itself. In the midst of the imperial escutcheons are to be seen the family arms of the Romanow and the Duke of Holstein, the two cross-beams of Oldenburg, the lion of Norway, the nettle leaf of Holstein, the lion of Schleswig, and others. And so at last we came once more to the Imperial residence, whose *comfortable* magnificence we had already seen, and at six o'clock, all the ceremonies being concluded, we hastened home to our well-earned dinner in Princess Trubetzkois' house.

Saturday, August 30.

A GRAND parade in the courtyard of the Kremlin before the Emperor. After it some equestrian performances took place. In the evening we were at the French theatre.

Sunday, August 31.

WE drove to the convent of St. Dimitri Donskoj, a complete fortress with battlemented walls and towers. The church is very beautiful, high, and unusually light; the Ikonostasis, which is covered with gold and pictures up to a hundred feet high, is of exceeding splendour. We heard mass, and had enough of the constant repetition of "*gospodi pomilui*" as the priest raised the bread high above his head and carried it through the Emperor's door; he shut this behind him and was seen through the golden lattice in a cloud of incense, the sparkling jewels of his tiara flashing here and there as he moved. Then there was a tinkling and some mysterious movements, after which the voices of the singers were heard as they began one of those wonderful melodies which in Russia alone can be heard in such perfection! Who could have expected to hear in this place such voices and such execution? We remained motionless till the singing ceased, the doors opened, and the priests displayed the miracle to the kneeling multitude.

To-day it is bright and sunny, very much like what we almost always have in Rome in December, only somewhat colder. Every one wears cloaks and furs, and if there came a little snow no one would be much surprised. We took advantage of this fine weather to drive to Sparrowhill. The Moskwa makes a beautiful bend here round another convent, the Djewitschi Monastery. It lies on the open "*Maiden's Meadow*," where the Emperor feasts all the "*black people*" after his coronation. On the other side lay Moscow in the sunshine, spread out in full beauty. So it must have looked to the French when, after such dreadful hardships, they expected this city to afford them rest and peace, and comfortable quarters for the winter. Three days later and all was covered with a sea of flames, and Napoleon fled from the Kremlin to Petrowskoi.

After breakfast we visited the strangest church in Moscow, that of Ivan Blajennoj, and then "*Redeemer's Church*," the most beautiful in all Russia, which is still in process of building. It is large and light, which can hardly be said of any other. The cupola is eighty feet in diameter. In the evening I went by command to visit the Empress-Mother at Alexandrinik. This palace is on the Moskwa, and quite in the city, though almost a mile from our quarter. The Empress held a Court, and Prince Friedrich Wilhelm, Prince Hohenzollern, Adlerberg, and I were invited. Only the few persons who were expressly invited to do so took seats in the presence of the Empress—the others all remained in the saloon. Her Majesty, in white muslin, dressed, as usual, very simply but elegantly, sat in an arm-chair, with her feet on a little stool. The conversation was quite unconstrained. It was pleasant to see how the *mamma* rejoiced in her youngest stripling son, the last who remained under her roof. Sometimes he had something to ask, sometimes a little joke to make, and the features of the Empress, though always grave, were full of benevolence and goodness. Her manner reminds one very much of her late father.

Monday, September 1.

LAST night it froze hard, and people were afraid for the orange-trees in the conservatories. I had the gigantic stove in my room heated a little, for the thermometer showed only seven degrees of heat, and you know how I hate this temperature.

At twelve o'clock we drove towards Petrowskoi, where there was a grand review of the army. The troops stood in six lines and the Emperor rode with his enormous retinue along the whole front. At the march past there were present in troops and regiments—

> 63,560 men Infantry.
> 9,740 ,, Cavalry.
> 1,700 ,, Artillery, with 136 guns.
> ―――
> 75,000 men.

This is the body-guard and a division of grenadiers. If these troops had been set out in one line they would have extended one German mile (four English), and though they stood in battalions they reached a very considerable distance.

The Empress was in a tent in front of which the march past took place; the Infantry in battalion columns, the Cavalry in squadrons, and the Artillery in batteries. It lasted about two hours and a half. There was a cutting wind which covered us with dust, and which must have been very injurious to the embroidered uniforms. After the march past the columns of cavalry were placed close to one another and then formed a line of about 2,000 feet long at a distance of about 800 feet from the spectators. The Emperor rode forward, and at his command this mass of quite 10,000 horse dashed forward at full gallop right down in front of where we were standing, where the halt was called.

That the troops should have returned from such long marches in full war strength I should have thought hardly possible.

There is now a Court dinner every day at the Kremlin, and then we go to the Theatre. The Opera House, which is just rebuilt, the old one having been destroyed by fire, was re-opened to-day. It is as broad as the one at Berlin, but has not quite so much depth.

It is, however, much more lofty, and has six tiers of boxes, one over another. The whole is white, with a great deal of gilding and red draperies. The Imperial box is roomy and richly decorated, but the ceiling, on the contrary, is so poor that I believe it to be only provisionally finished. The stage is very roomy, but the decorations and lighting only tolerable. Moscow has at present no gas, as there is a want of coal, of which, however, there are rich fields within 100 miles of the city.

They gave us Bellini's "*Puritani*" with Lablache and Bosio.

Tuesday, September 2.

THE whole day has been taken up with presentations. The entire diplomatic corps presented themselves to the prince, Count Morny, Prince Esterhazy, Lord Granville, Prince de Ligne as envoys, then the other ambassadors, with all their attachés in court dress and in splendid equipages, arrived. The prince, attended by all his suite, received them in great state. With the ease of manner which is peculiar to him, and assisted by his prodigious memory for persons and circumstances, he knew how to say something suitable to each of them. As a refreshment, we afterwards climbed up the great Hans, Ivan Weliki, from whence there is a very extended view. But we contented ourselves with stopping half way up, where we could see over all the churches and courts of the Kremlin. What lies beyond the city, too, is not beautiful, chiefly woods. I escaped from the dinner, and took a delightful walk round the walls of the Kitai-gorod. These walls are of enormous strength, with very high machicolated battlements, which command the very foot of the walls. Great towers stand like bulwarks before them. They are quite impregnable for Tartars.

In the evening we saw the wearisome "Gisela" danced, then about ten o'clock we went to the ball at the English ambassador's. In the morning by six o'clock we shall go to see the famous Troitzki Convent, seventy versts from here.

Wednesday, September 3.

AT six o'clock this morning we had already started in five carriages-and-four. It was the finest, warmest day we have yet had in Russia. The country is tolerably pretty and cultivated. In some fields oats, rye, and buckwheat are still standing, in others the winter seed is already a hand high. There is no time to be lost here, for winter may come very suddenly. The villages consist of little wooden houses, but they almost always have a fine church with a green cupola, so that they look pretty from a distance. There are generally also the tall chimneys of the cloth or sugar manufactories.

A newly-built rather important aqueduct surprised me very much; it brings drinking water to Moscow from a distance of several miles. The country is formed of low flat hills, and the only variety is afforded by occasional little valleys caused by streams. We made the distance to Troitzka in little more than four hours and a quarter, although it is ten miles off (forty English miles).

The Convent of Troitzka is of especial sanctity and historical importance, for on two occasions the deliverance of Russia from the Tartar and the Polish yoke issued from this convent. Neither these nations nor the French in 1812 entered it. It is true that it lay quite out of the line of the operations of the Emperor Napoleon, but still the Russians ascribe its safety to the wonder-working portrait of Saint Sergius, who is buried here. This picture was, they told me, removed to Sebastopol, but it was not able to prevent the place from being taken. There is not much to be seen in the way of architecture here. The finest thing is the very thick, high wall which, with its fortified towers, defends this little fortress. It has withstood the Polish guns in a siege. The Kolokol is something like the tower of the Catholic Church in Dresden, and contains very fine large bells. They took us on two versts farther to visit the Convent of Grottoes, *mais l'affaire ne valait pas la chandelle.* In returning, the carriage I was in ran into one of the others; the four miserable little horses which are harnessed to these carriages are not very easy to stop, and are accustomed to set off at once in full gallop. Both the Iswostschicks were ambitious to get first over a small bridge which had no balustrade and was only provided with a hand-rail, so we clashed together exactly in the middle of the bridge. Two of the horses fell into the ditch, some of the harness was broken, and the axle of my carriage was bent. But such things are of common occurrence here. We tied up the broken straps with string, and set off again at full gallop. By seven o'clock in the evening we got back, dined, and I was in time to hear the end of "*I Puritani.*"

Thursday, September 4.

AT the levée of the Austrian ambassador, Prince Esterhazy, who has fitted up his house in very fine style. Such a house costs here twenty thousand silver roubles for six weeks. We met Prince Schwarzenberg, Apponyi, Chotek, and many other Austrian gentlemen.

An excursion to the Convent of Simonofki showed us another fortress at the edge of the city, from which there is a splendid view. Then Von Werther gave us a very elaborate dinner, Lord Granville, Count Kissileff, Prince Gortschakoff, Adlerberg, Berg, Tolstoj, Woodhouse, Suworoff, etc. The last is a noble, genial man; he wears the order of the Annunciata which he has inherited from his father, the celebrated Suworoff whom this order raised to be *cousin du roi*.

We then drove to the Grand Duchess Helena's, and thence to a ball at Lord Granville's.

Friday, September 5.

AT nine o'clock we went to the spacious market on the south side of the high walls of the Kremlin, called the "*Rothen Platz*," or the Red Square. It originally formed the glacis of this fortress, and the battlements and towers of the old Czar's palace frown down upon it. In later times the merchants settled here, and the view extends along the whole northern side of the beautiful façade of the Gostinnoj Dwor and the great bazaar in the Chinese quarter. On the east side is the singular church, Blajennoj, with its numerous cupolas and towers, and on the west side there is the entrance through two arches under the gate tower, in front of which is the much-frequented chapel of the Iberian Madonna. In the middle the statue of the Burgher Minin is seated, and giving the sword into the hand of Prince Posharski to deliver his country from Polish rule. As soon as the great Ivan struck the hour, two heralds richly dressed, carrying gold staves, with shields and helmets, passed through the *Saint Saviour's* door (one of them unfortunately had his nose ornamented with a pair of spectacles). They were followed by twenty fine white horses with heavy trappings of cloth-of-gold, on which were embroidered the imperial eagles. The horses were led by grooms magnificently dressed, covered with gold lace, who bore printed proclamations. Two squadrons of cuirassiers with blaring trumpets closed the procession, which marched to the bronze statue of Posharski. The heralds proclaimed the approaching coronation of the new Emperor of all the Russias, scattered the proclamations amongst the people, and went on their way through the city.

We rode into the camp of the infantry and foot artillery; the cavalry is in cantonments. This town under canvas, with its fifty thousand inhabitants, has broad regular streets: it is placed on a treeless plain, and is very well suited for its purpose. Fourteen of these military monks sleep in one cell; they lie on wooden beds, with a little straw, and cover themselves with their long grey cloaks. Their knapsack is their pillow, and their arms stand in the middle of the tent, each of which is surrounded by a little wall of earth; the trench thus formed is very useful, but in excessive rain the water finds its way in from above. The month of July had been so cold that they had lighted enormous fires, but they were continually put out by the rain. Now, on the contrary, everything is covered with dust. Every droschky whirls up a cloud, as if a cavalry regiment were trotting by, and yet this dreary waste is preferred to the barracks.

The food is very good; each man has three pounds of good black bread a day, baked by the companies themselves, and half a pound of meat. Sauer-kraut soup and buck-wheat groats are their favourite luxuries. Dinner is eaten in the open air in companies, planks being used for forms, and weather not being taken into consideration. When asked, the men answered loudly and all together, like a battalion salvo, that they were doing very well; but they were very quiet, no singing or joking as among our men. They like to get behind the camp where their superiors, of whom they stand in awe, do not come. Then they sit down on the ground in their much-loved cloaks and talk till the Cossacks drive them away.

Paternal authority is the basis of all legal power in Russia. However unjust and hard a father may be, his injustice and his hardness does not overthrow his divine right. The Russian must above all things have a master; if he has not one, he seeks one for himself. The parish chooses a starost from among the oldest men; without him it would be like a swarm of bees without a queen. "Our country is good, but we have no head; come and reign over us," was the message they sent to Ruric. And the Warägers came from Norway and ruled for centuries till the usurper Boris Godunow had the last descendant of Ruric assassinated. The little Dimitri, a boy of six years—the only real Dimitri, and not one of the pretenders who were afterwards brought forward,—is laid in a richly ornamented coffin, in the church of Archangel at the Kremlin. They open the coffin on fête days. Every Russian who enters the church kneels before the dried-up body of the child who had been his little father; and although this child had never exercised the power, he none the less receives the homage of all Russia, even to the present day. Boris, the powerful ruler, the conqueror of the Tartars, the friend of the clergy, who had filled the churches and convents with gold and jewels, has not found a place in this long series of the tombs of the Czars. We saw his simple tomb at the Convent of Troitzka: the clergy have buried their benefactor outside their church. His likeness even is not to be found in the long series of Czars, on the gilded walls of Archangelski, where Ivan the Terrible rests in peace beside his murdered son, as if nothing had happened. The Romanoffs are the alone surviving descendants, by a daughter of the race of Ruric, and a daughter of Romanoff brought the sceptre of Russia to a prince of the house of Holstein.

And so with the soldiers. They would be in the greatest distress without their captain. Who would look after them, lead them, punish them? They may, perhaps, think that he has appropriated their property or ill-treated them in anger, but they love him more even than the Germans do, who are chastised with justice and deliberation. If a European soldier saw his officer in a state of drunkenness, there would be an end of discipline; but a Russian soldier puts him to bed, wipes off the dust, and obeys him in the morning when he has slept himself sober, with the same devotion as before.

The Russian peasants are naturally good-humoured and peaceable. I have never seen the people fighting or wrestling. They have no bull-fights or cock-fights. But their feeling for their superiors makes them, much against their inclination it is true, most submissive soldiers. During the flood in Petersburg sentries were drowned because they had not been discharged from their posts. As the Winter Palace was burning, a priest rescued the sacred vessels from the chapel. In the corridor he found a sentinel and told him the danger of remaining longer at his post. "*Prikass*!" (Orders) said the man; received absolution, and was burnt.

Historical portraits are always interesting. Even when they have in themselves no value as works of art, it seems possible to read the fate and the deeds of great personages in their features. Who can fail to be interested, if after following the history of Charles the First of England, he contemplates the noble, melancholy expression which Van Dyke knew how to depict in his portrait at Windsor. So Charles looked whilst witnessing the execution of Strafford, and there is the noble brow which daunted his accusers when he demanded to be judged by his peers. When we observe the statue of the Emperor Maximilian at Innspruck, the expressive countenance of Charles the Fifth, or the pale, fair youth Philip II., we see that the protruding underlip of the later Hapsburghers is inherited, but it is strange that this peculiarity passed over to the Lothringian family, although the noble and beautiful Maria Theresa did not share it.

Here in Djewuschka Convent we found a portrait of Natalie Narischkin, the mother of Peter the Great. She was of Tartar origin, and there is a singular likeness to the Emperor Paul, to whom she was but slightly related.

In this convent Peter the Great shut up his step-sister and co-regent Sophia, because she was continually exciting the Strelitzes and Old Russians to resist his innovations. Here she had her lover Chabauski nailed by his hands to a window which is still pointed out, and here she died in the greatest sanctity. As a sign that she really was the legitimate ruler, her portrait bears the double eagle with St. George, which specially indicates the Czars who conquered the Infidels.

"*Voilà Rome tartare,*" cried Madame de Stael as she looked on Moscow. If she had said *Rome russe* it would have been less clever but more true. Moscow and the Kremlin are exactly the opposite of the Tartar spirit and the palpable expression of the genuine and pure Russian spirit.

As I walked to-day along the beautiful granite quay by the side of the Moskwa, a discharged soldier begged alms from me. He had been crippled by a shot, perhaps at Sebastopol, and now he was a free man, that is, his former feudal lord had now no claim upon him, as he was no longer a serf, and for the same reason he had no longer a share in the property of the commune. Had be been married at the time when, amid the lamentations of his relations, he was seized for military service, when his hair was cut off, and he was carried off, the State would put his children into the foundling hospital, and after three years his wife could legally marry another man. If he were now to return to his native village on the Ural or on the White Sea, he would find in it, after being away for fifteen years, no one who belonged to him, but a new generation, and the graves of his relations; while he himself is a stranger without rights, a beggar who not only cannot work, but must not work. This is the freedom of the discharged soldier. Russia was till lately the only European state which had no proletariate. In consequence of the most peculiar constitution of the communes in which communism and socialism have actually existed for centuries, and where private property and inheritance have no existence, there may be poor communes but no very poor individuals. Every Russian has a home somewhere, and there he has a share in the soil of the commune. As long as the law imposing twenty-five years' military service was rigorously carried out, the soldier, of course, generally remained with his regiment till he died. The few who were discharged perished unnoticed. But when the period of service was reduced to twelve or fifteen years, then it was a different matter. In the first place, the army requires almost double the amount of compensation that it had before. The wealth of the nobles is here reckoned by the number of "*souls*" they possess; each such "soul" is a valuable property paying tribute to the feudal lord, who is a greater loser now than he was formerly, because the distressing grievance of levying recruits occurs much oftener, and is more extensive than formerly. The large number of discharged soldiers, amounting annually to 50,000 men, helps to form a proletariate race, to which also the rapid increase of the manufacturing interest largely contributes. Dreading work, and incapable of work, often addicted to drink, these discharged soldiers are still of an age to marry. No doubt the new ruler will endeavour to find some remedy for this state of things, but it will be no easy task, for it necessitates reforms everywhere, and that in a country which dislikes everything new.

And now there stood a man who, not many months before, had shed his blood for his country, begging an alms, within sight of the Kremlin, the very heart of the Empire which owes, and will always owe, its greatness to its faithful, conscientious, brave, and long-enduring soldiers. Truly, paradise must await these patient ones!

The newly made "*free-man*," in his long, grey cloak, his cap humbly removed, went his way into "holy" Russia, and we—we drove in imperial carriages to a grand dinner.

Saturday, September 6.

TO-DAY the Prince received fifty or sixty different princes from Grussia, Mingrelia, Kurdistan, Caucasia, Tscherkessia etc. etc., all in the national costume, with jewels and gold stuffs, Persian caps and richly ornamented weapons.

They tell of one of the Tscherkesses, who being asked at a ball if his pistols were loaded, replied, "Why should I carry pistols if they were not loaded?" A Kurd, with whom I managed to have some conversation in Turkish, had also a loaded pistol, but he showed me that he had no powder in the pan. The company had a very picturesque appearance, and formed a great contrast to the assembly at the Sardinian ambassador's, to which we drove immediately afterwards.

Sunday, September 7.

THE sky has favoured this festival with splendid weather. By seven o'clock in the morning the city looked quite deserted, for everyone had hastened to the Kremlin, although the doors were not to be opened till eight o'clock.

In their Majesties' ante-chambers we found a host of chamberlains covered with gold, and the highest functionaries of the Court with their staves of eight feet long, and all the ladies in their national costume. The colours of their robes depend on their different courts, scarlet with gold, silver, blue, amaranth, etc. etc., so that, although there is an uniformity of shape, there is a pleasant variety of colour. The head-dress, too, is ornamented with gold, diamonds, coloured stones, or pearls, according to the taste and means of the individual.

One single chair was secretly used in turn by some very old ladies; they had certainly been standing since seven, and probably they had been working hard at their grand toilettes since four o'clock in the morning.

At nine o'clock the doors of the imperial

began to move, and the Dowager Empress appeared, supported by her two youngest sons. She wore a crown entirely of diamonds, a mantle of gold stuff and ermine, the train of which was borne by six chamberlains, and which was fastened by a splendid chain of diamonds. Her slender figure, her cameo profile, her stately bearing, and the sweet gravity of her expression, excited the involuntary admiration of everyone. The evening before, she had assembled all her children to give them her blessing. After her came the heir to the throne, the Grand Dukes and Grand Duchesses, Prince Friedrich Wilhelm, Prince Friedrich of the Netherlands, Alexander of Hesse, and the rest of the princes of royal houses, then their suites, and behind us the ladies.

The *cortège* passed through Alexander's Hall, the Wladimir and George's halls, a length of more than 500 feet. On the left were drawn up some grenadiers, the guards, the cuirassiers with glittering armour, deputations from the cavalry regiments, and the infantry, all with standards and colours and shining arms. On the right stood all the officers.

The Empress passed down the great open stairs into the court of the old Palace of the Czars, and there a baldaquin of gold stuff awaited her, which was borne over her by eight of the chamberlains with the long staves. The streaming out of the procession into the bright sunshine was a splendid sight.

Behind the lines of troops stood the people, bearded men, with heads uncovered, close together, but without any confusion. The open space is surrounded by three grand churches of the Ascension, Archangel, and the Annunciation, with the church of Ivan Weliki and a high trellis work of iron. The platforms for spectators, covered with red cloth, were half as high as the buildings, and there sat lords and ladies gaily dressed. Now clashed the countless bells of Moscow, but deeper than them all boomed the great Wetschewoj, the monster bell from Novgorod, which was heard above all the blaring of the trumpets and the continual cheering of the multitude. Only the artillery could be heard above the din.

When I had reached the bottom of the stairs, I succeeded in turning round to take a look at the magnificent procession of the ladies behind us. The diplomatic corps had already arrived at Uspenski Sabor, and we took our places by their side on a platform without seats, which ran along three sides of this great church. The fourth side is formed by the Ikonostasis, behind which is the altar. The throne was placed opposite to this, and had two seats; it was raised somewhat from the ground, and had over it a splendid baldaquin. The Dowager Empress had a seat on the right of the throne, the princes stood behind on the left.

The church, as I said before, is small, and only holds a very limited number of spectators, but perfect order reigned throughout. The sun shone brightly, streaming through the windows, and reflecting itself in all the gilding which covers walls and pillars to the highest point of the cupola, and making it so bright that, being very well placed, I had an excellent view of all the proceedings.

First of all came the regalia, borne by the highest civil and military officers, the imperial banner with the double eagle, brought from Byzantium, the imperial seal, a steel plate the size of a hand, without engraving or ornament, the sword of the Empire, the coronation robes for their Majesties, the golden ball or globe (Severin carried this ball on a cushion of cloth-of-gold), the girdle of large diamonds, the sceptre with the great diamond Lazaref— one of the largest known diamonds,—and lastly the two crowns. That of the Emperor is formed of diamonds, with a row of the largest pearls, and has a cross with a ruby of matchless value in it. This stone is an inch long, about half an inch wide, and a quarter of an inch thick, but irregular in form, and uncut. When the sun fell upon the crown with all its diamonds, it was reflected and sparkled with every colour. The Empress's crown is like it but smaller, and it seemed not to be easy to keep on the head, although it was fastened on with diamond hairpins.

And now the cross was taken out of the church to meet the Emperor, who was approaching, and the Metropolitan of Moscow sprinkled his path with holy water. Their Majesties bowed three times at the door, and took their seats on the throne, the priests stood between the throne and the middle door of the Ikonostasis, and the choir chanted the Psalm "*Misericordiam.*" Of the touching beauty of the Russian church melodies I have told you before; they were performed by men's voices only, without any instrumental accompaniment. They are all ancient melodies, mostly introduced from the West, but are as far removed from the meagre hymns of Protestantism as from the operatic music of the Catholic Church. The singers are extraordinarily well trained, and incredibly fine bass voices are heard, which in this limited space were re-echoed with marvellous power from the walls and cupolas.

Since Peter the Great incorporated the patriarchal with the imperial power, the Metropolitan of Moscow is the principal ecclesiastic of this vast Empire; at the present time he is a fine-looking but very aged man, Philaretes by name—the same who crowned the Emperor Nicolas. Much stress is laid on the fine bass voices of the superior clergy; the voice of the old Metropolitan could hardly be heard as he requested the Emperor to recite his belief. This being done, the Emperor put on the coronation robes, which are made of the richest gold stuff, lined with ermine. He bowed himself and remained in that position, whilst the Metropolitan laid his hand on his head and said two long blessings. Then the crown was brought to the Emperor, and he himself put it on his head, grasped the sceptre with his right hand, the ball with his left, and so sat down on the throne. Then the Empress came and knelt before him. The Emperor took the crown from his head and put it on hers; she was then dressed in the crown and mantle, and seated herself on the throne on the left hand of her husband.

It was impressive to see how the aged, stately Empress-mother followed all these movements with eager attention. Her youngest son showed much anxiety to support her, and to draw more closely her ermine furs, lest she should feel the cold. The wife of an American diplomatist, near me fainted away, and the Princess Helena fell into her husband's arms, but the Emperor's aged mother stood it all out bravely. She rose and advanced with a firm step to the foot of the throne, the sparkling crown on her head and the mantle of gold brocade trailing behind. Here, before all the world, she embraced her firstborn and blessed him. The Emperor kissed her hands. Then all the grand dukes and princes followed, bowing low; and the Emperor embraced them. Whilst all this was going on, *Domine salvum fac Imperatorem* was sung, the bells in all the churches rang out, a hundred cannon shook the windows, and all the spectators bowed three times.

Next, the Emperor, divested of his imperial robes, stepped down from the throne and knelt in prayer—all the company kneeling or bending low in prayer for the welfare of their new monarch.

In the hand of no mortal is such unlimited power laid as in that of this man, who is the absolute ruler of the tenth part of the inhabitants of the earth, whose sceptre stretches over four quarters of the world, and who lays his commands on Christians and Jews, Mussulmans and heathen. Who can fail to pray God, that His grace may enlighten the man whose will is law to 60,000,000 people, whose word is obeyed from the Wall of China to the Vistula, from the Polar Sea to Mount Ararat, to whose call half a million of soldiers are obedient, and who even now (1856) has given peace to Europe? May he be victorious in the peaceful conquests he is about to attempt in the interior of his vast kingdom, and remain a firm supporter of law and order!

After this came the "*Te Deum*" and the exceedingly long mass according to the Greek rites.

When it was ended the Emperor descended the steps of the throne, laid aside his robes and arms, and entered the holy of holies by the Emperor's door, and kneeling before the altar received the sacrament in both kinds as well as the priests. The Empress partook of the same in the Greek manner, in front of the door. Then followed the anointing with oil on the forehead, eyelids, lips, ears, breast, and hands, by the Metropolitan, who used a costly vessel. The bishops of Novgorod and Moscow wiped away the oil. Their Majesties now re-seated themselves on the throne, putting on again the crowns, robes, and the great diamond chain of the order of Alexander Newski. From this moment they are the Lord's anointed, and the ceremony was concluded.

The Emperor and Empress next went to the neighbouring churches, Archangel and Blagowestchenski. From my place at the top of the stairs I saw the young Emperor as he came out of the church. He walked in front of the baldaquin with the sceptre and the imperial globe in his hands. The crown blazed in the sunshine on his head, the mantle of gold and ermine trailed far behind, over the steps covered with crimson cloth. After him followed an endless train of lords and ladies, forming a most brilliant procession. He continually saluted the cheering multitude on both sides, although the heavy crown hardly permitted him to bend his head.

There were the representatives of twenty different peoples in their Oriental costumes, curious travellers from every corner of Europe, and the bearded Muschiks from "holy" Russia. Even on the other side of the Moskwa the people stood as close as possible. They could not see anything which passed behind the walls of the Kremlin, but the shouts from within, the ringing of the bells, the thunder of the guns, and the fanfare of the music, told them that their

Czar, their Batuschka, was now crowned and anointed.

The Emperor looked grave but kindly: he seemed to feel the whole significance of the ceremony, not because of its extraordinary splendour, but in spite of it. And it would not be easy to see anything more brilliant than this fairy-like city spread out in the sunshine, filled with everything which is rich and grand, from far and near, with the long procession winding between ancient monuments and sacred edifices, bearing the treasures of the church, the weapons of the army, and the regalia of the state, to greet the new Emperor.

Next came the banquet at Granowitaja Palata, the ancient residence of the Czars. Under a magnificent canopy of gold brocade lined with ermine, stood three chairs and a table for their Majesties, who seated themselves, still wearing their crowns. The other tables were laid as they are seen at the theatre, only on one side, so that no one turned his back on the throne. After the Emperor had laid aside the regalia, he called for wine, and drank to the health of his faithful subjects. The ambassadors retired backwards out at the door, only the superior clergy and the highest functionaries took their places at table, which groaned under the weight of many hundred-weight of ancient silver plate, gigantic goblets, vessels, ewers, and dishes, rather rudely fashioned, but massive and quaint.

The ceremony ended with this banquet, and the solemn procession through the palaces about four o'clock in the afternoon. We had been eight hours on our legs without sitting down for one moment. There were innumerable tables set out for us in tents erected for the purpose, but we drove back and enjoyed our dinner at home.

In the evening the city was illuminated. I both drove and walked through the surging crowd, and I could not but admire the intelligence, docility, and quietness of the men; indeed there cannot be a more harmless, good-natured people than the common Russian people.

In Russia the soil belongs to the people, but the communes have the usufruct, and they cannot alienate their fields or any part of them. No individual can be a proprietor, but every member of the commune has an equal right with all the others to the use of it. This right is common for woods and pasturage, but the fields, on the contrary, are divided into exactly so many parcels as there are male members of the commune; and since this condition changes, there is a new division every ten or fifteen years. In the villages measuring-rods are kept which are considered sacred, and they are shorter in proportion, for good land, and longer for bad. Each household receives a share of the land proportionate to the number of its male members; waste pieces and corners are held in reserve for any compensation or re-adjustment required in the intervals. Disputes are settled by the unlimited authority of the starosts or elders, who are elected by the communes themselves.

This very ancient but still existing state of things has consequences which are most noteworthy. Except the Pelowniks or Halbbauern, who are of Tschudisch (Finnish) origin, there is in Russia no private property in land, for anyone. The free communes are the proprietors, the crown communes are occupiers, the nobles are tenants. Within the communes there are only usufructuaries. There exists no such thing as the inheritance of land. The son does not inherit his father's fields; he receives his share not on the ground of inheritance, but in virtue of his birth as a member of the commune. Every Russian has a settlement somewhere, and there are no poor people, no proletariate. No one is quite poor. A father may run through everything; his children do not inherit his poverty. The increase of the family, which is with us such a source of anxiety, is, in Russia, an increase of wealth. Everything favours early marriages. The entrance into the family of even the poorest daughter-in-law is made a festival. She brings with her a pair of laborious hands, and a parcel of land is laid aside for her sons from the day of their birth.

On the other hand it must be confessed, that by this division of the land, no part of it is kept in a state of perfection. Who will make improvements, plant trees, make drains on a piece of land, which, after fifteen years will perhaps belong to some one else?

Personally the Russian *Bauer* was quite free. Nobility is not an institution of Russian origin: it is, as in England, of German origin; the Normans, who in 860 came over with Ruric, brought it with them. Neither were they strictly feudal lords of the land, but the peasants living in a certain district were obliged to pay them rent. This rent, called obrok, was very moderate at first, and could not be increased, lest the extreme poverty of the payer should prevent him from paying anything at all. Boris Godenow first raised this tax in 1580, and in the Russian popular songs, lamentations on this subject still exist. The bondage of the peasants first appeared in the time of Peter the Great: until his time only prisoners of war had been made slaves or serfs. The peasant either served the lord personally in the house, or he paid the obrok and cultivated the fields. The lord had to provide for his maintenance if he became destitute or incapable of work. He could, indeed, sell him, but not without the land: his dependants who were annexed to it were like an encumbrance. He could not sell the land, he could sell only the rent paid by the people who lived on the land, and to whom the usufruct belonged. The noble himself hardly ever resided on the land. There are no castles and fortified houses such as those in which our knights took such firm root, and whose names still survive. The Russian noble lived and still lives mostly in the cities, either in Moscow or Petersburg. "On dit que j'aye de superbes terres du côte de Tomsk!" one of them was heard to say. An adjutant of the Emperor, being sent on duty to the Volga, and finding the country charming, waited some time, and then inquired who was the owner of that property? The answer was his own name. It is as if we had a hypothec on a property which we have never seen, and with the management of which we have nothing to do. Peter the Great gave the real estate to the nobles, a boundless gift—half of all the cultivated land in Russia; while the usufruct remained with the peasants. And further, he removed Russia from the list of mere agricultural states, by founding the first manufactories. To these whole communes were assigned, which all worked for the manufactory, and in return the manufactory was charged with their support. So first originated the idea that the serf could be employed according to the will of his owner. A serf received permission to migrate, and might become a celebrated artist, or merchant, or millionaire. But let the noble raise the obrok to thousands of roubles, he can forbid the man to marry, can order him back to his property, etc. etc. The manufactories have increased enormously since 1825. Their business requires constant vigilance; the presence of the proprietor is necessary; he must live on his property, and therefore the obrok is exchanged for personal service. The peasant receives half or two-thirds of the fields, and must moreover attend to the portion of his lord, who perhaps is a *parvenu*, and has no patriarchal feelings at all.

Everyone feels that serfdom is in opposition to the increase of civilisation, and cannot continue, but the great difficulty is how to alter it. If liberty were suddenly given to four-and-twenty millions of peasants, agriculture would come to an end in the least fertile parts of the kingdom. There are at most only five months in which to plough, sow, and reap; by the 6th of August the winter seed must already be sowed. Agriculture is then set aside to some extent, since the man has the other seven months in which to speculate, trade, or work at some handiwork. The culture of the fields only produces corn, which in good years is worth but little, whilst, on the contrary, the wages paid in manufactories are as high as those paid in England. A weaver earns daily a bushel of corn in East Russia, in Bielefield scarcely three-quarters of a bushel. The more the manufactures increase, the more difficult the case will become. Where they do not exist, the obrok is insignificant, leaving twenty times as large a sum to turn into capital. But who can decide the right of a lord to the obrok of a great singer, or merchant, or speculator, or millionaire? Serfdom was abolished with us, and it must disappear here where they have to do with communes instead of with individuals. For it must be taken for granted, that the ancient institution of communes cannot be altered; in spite of its ill effect on agriculture it has inestimable advantages in its social relations, and is capable of a wider development.

The Russian commune arranges its own affairs through officers elected from among themselves, the Starosts, whom it obeys unhesitatingly. The Imperial officials are unhappily often notoriously untrustworthy and corrupt. The young Emperor has already endeavoured to put down this evil with a strong hand, but it is very deep-rooted. With them to be caught in a fraud is a misfortune, not as with us a disgrace. Too many are interested in abuses. The fewer, therefore, there are of such officials the better.

The means of self-government is given not only to the communes but also to the nobles, who were constituted a corporate body, under their "*marschalls*," by Katharine II., but they have at present made very little use of it.

No aristocracy less than the Russian answers its real and proper purpose of asserting and maintaining its own independence, both against the imperial power and the power of the commons. There is indeed a real and ancient nobility; the Trubetzkoi, the Gagarin, etc. etc., who date their family from Ruric, even from Odin! But these hereditary nobles are quite swamped by the official nobility: for whereas in all other countries nobility proceeds from the will of the monarch, in Russia it is attained according to a certain law. The sons of certain officials become *ipso facto* ennobled. Everyone who reaches the rank of the fifth class attains at once hereditary nobility; and, what is more, the most ancient nobility is forfeited if the possessor has not attained in three generations some rank in the service of the State. For this reason the nobles are entirely dependant on the government, and it is not easy for them to oppose it in any way. Not that this should be their object, but with the possibility. disappears also their whole importance. Certainly the stronger, the healthier, and more independent the people are from their communal constitution, and the more influential the spiritual power is, the less can the Government afford to let the nobility with their boundless possessions in land withdraw from its influence. But in England there is both the self-government of the commons and the power and wealth of the nobility. An English "nobleman" owes all his greatness to his birth, the service of the State adds nothing to it. An English viscount, who may be Prime Minister or Lieutenant-General is below an earl or duke who may be only an ensign, or nothing at all. Whether this would suit Russia I cannot decide, but where it does not exist there is no aristocracy in the political sense of the word.

Neither is there here any *bourgeoisie*. The first class of merchants belongs to the rank of nobles, those below them are "Mushiks," although often millionaires, and belong to the same grade of culture with the peasants whom they resemble in dress and manners. The manufacturing interest is also quite in the hands of those nobles who are landholders.

The popes form a separate class: it is only their children who become popes, and these again marry (before ordination, and never a second time) only the daughters of popes. Their influence is very great, although they are quite as uncultivated as the peasants, who kiss their hands as being the bearers of the sacred symbols.

Russia falls, therefore, naturally into two unequal parts, the cultivated class and the *tschorni narod*, " *the black race* ;" the first of these numbers at the most half a million of men, while the last includes sixty millions.

Peter the Great could not wait to ennoble his people from the root; he grafted German and Dutch, and Katharine, French twigs on the topmost boughs. These bear now their southern fruit on a strong and healthy stem, and the wide-spreading branches have quite driven out the old crab-apple.

The Civilisation of the West so suddenly and violently introduced has never penetrated the lower strata of society. A small number of fashionable Russians in stars and uniforms, educated in the French style, and brought up in the greatest luxury, exist side by side, and without any intermediate steps, with the mass of the strong, bearded, ignorant, but pious and docile people who exceed them in number a hundred-fold. It can hardly be believed that the small, refined, court gentleman, the elegant officer in the Guards, who speaks French like his mother-tongue, is of the same nation with the Iswoschtschik who drives his carriage, or the Mushik who waits at his door. In England all classes look much the same outwardly, and the peasants even wear no different costume, so that a general culture spreads through all classes, which compensates for the intellectual differences. In Russia all differences are brought into the most violent contrast: palaces close to hovels; splendid cities in desolate wastes; railways which extend for hundreds of miles without touching any towns but their termini; prairies where no corn will grow; over-refinement by the side of coarseness. Art is everywhere in conflict with Nature in the endeavour to wrest violently from her that which is demanded by the most exaggerated requirements. It must be conceded that the Russian Emperors have done wonders. One of the most splendid imperial cities has been raised amid the swamps of the Neva, although the stream itself threatens to engulph it, there are mighty fleets on a sea which is frozen for seven months of the year; an excellent army has been formed where each man is interest-paying capital to his master; there are museums containing the masterpieces of every country, where the people for hundreds of miles round only value the black pictures of saints; parqueted floors, but break-neck pavements in the streets; in short, rough contrasts everywhere.

It remains an important question whether they will advance on the road taken by Peter I., that is, propagate the civilisation of foreign lands and other climes, or whether they will endeavour to cultivate this docile and tractable people themselves from within.

The reaction against the direction which has been followed for the last fifty years has always existed, and is concentrated in Moscow. It was displayed in the war which has just ended, and has not been successful. It will be long before the Russians can dispense with the help of foreigners, that is, with the steadiness, the capacity, and the loyalty of the Germans, for only long years and an iron determination will make trustworthy Russian officials. Above all, the clergy must be won to educate themselves and to aid in the enlightenment of the people. Nothing must be done suddenly or violently, but the efforts of a century would be a small price to pay for a truly national Russian development.

Monday, September 8.

AT ten o'clock there was parade of the guard on the Kremlin, and in the evening a Polonaise ball in the palace, which was splendidly illuminated. The bands of music were placed in the saloons, which are wide enough to admit them without inconvenience. The ladies all wore trains. There must have been some thousand guests. Besides the rich military uniforms, there were many Orientals in their different national dresses, which gave the fête a peculiar character of its own; whereas such balls are generally all exactly alike.

The regalia were placed in St. Andrew's Hall on a table, and everyone could look at these treasures as closely as they pleased. This is not customary in a company so numerous and and so varied. I saw several people who did not hesitate to handle the different articles.

The Emperor opened the ball with his mother, and he danced afterwards with the Empress, the Grand Duchesses, the wives of the ambassadors, etc. etc. He must really have passed over a distance of several versts!

By eleven o'clock everything was over, and I was glad enough to find my carriage, and drive home through the illuminated city.

In the absence of gas, the illuminations were made entirely of candles. In London they would have used nothing but gas, which would have been laid on to each house provisionally. Here, of course, the light is far less intense, but very peculiar. In the little peep-shows, such as children have, one sees pictures in which the architectural lines are marked out by pin-holes, through which the light shines. Just so is it here with the houses and palaces. They have naturally decorated first those houses which the Emperor was to see. The court-yards through which he had to pass were as bright as day. The view was magnificent from the great terrace of St. George's Hall.

The fine houses on the other side of the Moskwa sparkled with countless lights, and in the still farther distance rose the masses of houses with their towers and cupolas. The most singular effect was produced by the Wassili-Blashen-noj, that strange church I have mentioned before, whose many cupolas being marked out in light, the wonderful outline fell directly on the eyes. But the light of these lamps is not strong enough to show the different colours from so great a distance; if it were lighted by Bengal lights this church would look fabulously beautiful. The loveliest of all was the Kremlin itself, seen from a distance. The many high towers and well-lighted white walls had a fairy-like effect. There was no wind to spoil the illuminations; the evening was perfectly calm and therefore mild. Everything so far has gone excellently well.

Tuesday, September 9.

TO-DAY at eleven o'clock there was a military court held; the great saloons were quite filled with officers in full dress.

The Russian army contains, including those who have retired, eight thousand generals, some hundreds of whom were certainly present. The Emperor alone had a hundred and eighty adjutants. Each of the guests went forward singly to make his bow, first to the Emperor, then to the Empress. The Emperor shook hands and said a few pleasant words to each one, the Empress gave her hand to each to kiss, and then we went out at the other end of the saloon, and so home. As there were certainly some thousands of officers to follow us, I thought of St. Peter at Rome, whose right toe is half kissed away, though it is made of bronze.

In the afternoon we visited the arsenal and the fine armour which is preserved there, as well as a number of ancient thrones, crowns, sceptres, and ornaments.

Wednesday, September 10.

PIERCING cold wind and dust. The imperial church choir sang at Lwoff.

Thursday, September 11.

THE Emperor's name-day, therefore the lords and ladies of the Court, and the officers all assembled in the Kremlin in great state, walking in procession through the saloons to the chapel to hear mass. Afterwards we had an audience to take leave of the Emperor, who bade us farewell in the most friendly manner.

The Empress did not receive us, being probably tired out, but the Dowager Empress took leave of us most kindly. She was in simple but costly morning dress, consisting of a white Indian shawl with a wide border; she sat, or rather lay on two arm-chairs. She chatted with each of us, and gave every one her hand to kiss. " I thought I should have died of joy and excitement at the coronation;" said she, "but I prayed so earnestly that God has preserved me."

Then we had an audience to take leave of the Grand Duchess of Weimar, the Grand Duchess Helena, and the Grand Dukes. In the evening there was a state opera. Besides the enormous lustre in the middle of the house, there were ninety-five crystal lustres, each of several lights, in front of the five rows of boxes. More than a thousand lights, and lords and ladies in the gayest dresses made a splendid sight. They gave us "Elisire d'amore" and a tedious ballet; the stage was dark and the decorations meagre, but—Cerito danced.

Friday, September 12.

THE day of departure. It rained. At twelve o'clock the Emperor came to take the Prince to see some infantry manœuvres which were to take place at Petrowskoj. The thermometer was almost at freezing point; a storm of wind drove the rain right into our faces. The troops waded in mire, and in the escort, consisting of several hundred cavalry, the epaulettes, embroidered uniforms, and stars, were all covered with mud. After four hours of this we returned, wet to the skin and frozen with cold.

After dinner there were still some farewell visits to make. The Emperor came to take leave of the Prince; he wore a general's uniform with the ribbon of the order of the black eagle. We received him in full dress, and he talked pleasantly to every one. Immediately afterwards the Prince drove to the Emperor.

In the evening we went once more to the theatre to take leave of some friends, and at twelve o'clock we set off in four carriages-and-four and a fourgon.

For the first two days it rained, and blew,

and was bitterly cold. The country is very dreary and desolate, and hardly any dwelling-houses were to be seen; it was mostly wood and uncultivated plains. There are provisions for sleeping at the post-houses.

The courier who preceded us provided for all our wants—coffee, tea, and dinner, which last we did not take till seven o'clock in the evening. The horses were always ready for us and were harnessed in two or three minutes, when we started again at full gallop. We generally accomplished about eight miles in the hour, but often more.

On the third day my carriage was broken, and had to be two hours in the smithy. I got into the *coupé* of the *fourgon* with Harry. In order to overtake the prince two more horses were put on in front, and we set off again at a tearing gallop. But as we came to a cross road the leader turned to go home to its native village, the Jamschtschik not being able to hold him, the carriage turned over and fell down the sloping bank of a dam almost six feet high, and lay there with its wheels uppermost. We all escaped without any great hurt. "*Semliaki*" (country people!) shouted the coachman, and quickly appeared some bearded Russians, who first turned the carriage over, and then with poles and levers they got it up and loaded and harnessed once more. The good fellows were surprised and delighted to find their services rewarded by the gift of a few roubles.

We had altogether 2,000 horses in the course of our journey to Warsaw, where we arrived at three o'clock in the morning, and were received, even at that inconvenient hour, by the authorities in grand style. There we took the rail for the remaining 480 miles. Altogether we were five days and six nights on the road, with no break but the two hours' sleep at Warsaw, and without taking off our clothes.

Printed by R. & R. CLARK, *Edinburgh.*

www.ingramcontent.com/pod-product-compliance
Lightning Source LLC
Chambersburg PA
CBHW030819190426
43197CB00036B/604